D1521022

the compleat Blueberry cookbook

the *compleat* Blueberry cookbook

ELIZABETH W. BARTON

Earliblue

PHOENIX PUBLISHING
Canaan, New Hampshire 03741

To Walter

Contents

PART ONE
All About Blueberries

PART TWO
And How to Serve Them

Acknowledgments

The author acknowledges with gratitude the advice of Dr. George M. Darrow (retired), for forty-six years a leading specialist in fruit research for the U.S. Department of Agriculture and recipient of the Wilder Medal and the Distinguished Service Medal of the U.S.D.A., who reviewed early chapters of this book. She also extends her appreciation to Dr. Arlen Draper, Research Geneticist, Plant Research Division, Agricultural Research Service, U.S. Department of Agriculture, Greenbelt, Maryland, for furnishing information used in portions of the chapters on blueberry culture and the history of the blueberry. To all of the kind friends who offered their favorite recipes for inclusion in the book, or who helped in testing those created in her kitchen, she offers her most heartfelt thanks.

"Why, there hasn't been time for the bushes to
    grow,
That's always the way with the blueberries,
    though:
There may not have been a ghost of a sign
Of them anywhere under the shade of the pine,
But get the pine out of the way, you may burn
The pasture all over until not a fern
Or grass-blade is left, not to mention a stick,
And presto, they're up all around you as thick
And hard to explain as a conjurer's trick."

Excerpt from "Blueberries,"
from *The Poetry of Robert Frost,*
edited by Edward Connery Lathem,
Holt, Rinehart and Winston,
New York, 1969

Foreword

Far up in the White Mountains of New Hampshire there is a special hill with two peaks at the summit. I live on one of them. This region is called the highest cultivated area in New Hampshire.

From the tiptop of my peak I can see two tree-rimmed lakes and two tiny towns, and, circling the whole, chains of mountains that reach out into limitless space, changing their colors with each hour of the day and in each season of the year.

In the mornings white clouds fill the valleys, making small tender islands of the other mountain peaks. This all-enveloping mist temporarily veils all living things like a mysterious, ephemeral lake without beginning or end. But one end I know. It's my cabin. As the pink-tinged mist clears away, our field appears and then the rows of birches beside the road, glistening in the yellowing sun, next the firs and maples that rim the stone wall at the foot of our slope, and eventually the farms and forests beyond, until I can see the white steeples of the churches in our town and the majestic glory of the mountains again.

In winter snow hides the secrets of that rolling field in front of my cabin, but as the ice breaks and the white meadow melts into spring, grasses and wild flowers distribute their lavish colors, and amongst them, in cunning profusion, the blueberry plants begin to spread their precise branches, their waxy white flowers giving way to tiny green nuggets of promise. As spring and summer progress, dark green, waxy leaves spread lavishly and the tiny green balls turn to magenta and mauve, and then in a burst, almost overnight it seems, they are gloriously big and round and unbelievably blue. Suddenly then our slope is a carpet of blue velvet, for our tiny, eager plants have found their way across every inch of ground, and it becomes a task to walk through the field without crushing some of them.

I lived for many years without tasting a blueberry. City-bred, I was middle-aged before I ever saw them growing wild, and then, amidst the delights of a late marriage, my husband took me up to this hilltop and told me it was his, and now mine. It was "blueberry time," and we filled a bucket with the wild, sweet fruit, still wet from the morning dew, and sat down against an old stone wall, and began to eat our fill. It was then that my love affair with the blueberry began. It is inevitably an element in my affection for New Hampshire and our own hill.

I love the plants in every season from their first brown struggles up from the ground and out of the snow to that last final hour in late September when the blue velvet carpet has turned a deep rich red. With them I rejoice in the first budding and flowering, and with them I suffer the shock of the final cutting of the field before winter, when all but their hardy roots are demolished. (In some places farmers burn the fields — say it's good for the next crop. I couldn't bear that!) I hate to see anyone pluck a blueberry before the plants are ripe. On our hill this occurs no sooner than August. I hate to see anyone step on a plant, or pick the berries carelessly, or take more than they need. I think they *know!*

But we are rich in blueberries, and so we share them, and cook them, and eat them. Since they must be used, I like to think that they are used with delight and in good health, and so I wish to share with you what I have learned about the nurturing and cooking of blueberries.

ELIZABETH W. BARTON
Fieldcrest Cottage
Whitefield, New Hampshire
May, 1974

PART ONE

All about Blueberries

Bluecrop

History of the Blueberry

Blueberries in the wild state grow in many parts of the world. They are known as far south as the tropics and as far north as the Arctic Circle. Commercially, their cultivation has been generally confined to the North American Continent, but in recent years some planting has been done in Central Europe.

In early American references to the berry, it was most often called a "hurtleberry," although "bilberry," "whortleberry," "whinberry," and "trackleberry," were terms also used because such were the names applied to the English species of the plant with which the writers were familiar. The Scots called them "blaeberries," "blae" in their dialect meaning blackish-blue.

Blueberry jam, made from the wild berry, has been used in Scotland from the time of James V for spreading on the popular Scottish scones. The berry is highly esteemed by the Danes and the Russians as food, and is considered an important part of the diet of many Eskimos.

On our continent, explorers early noted the edibility of the wild berry, its abundance, and its importance to the diet of the American Indian. The Indians, they found, harvested the wild crops, traded, and sold them, and used them frequently in their cooking — besides eating them raw. To prolong their use to the winter months, they raised scaffolds of rush mats and dried the berries.

One of the first North American explorers to mention this berry in his journals was Samuel de Champlain who, in 1615, reached Lake Huron and reported finding Indians there gathering blueberries for their winter store. He noted that they beat dried berries into powder, added it to parched meal, and thus produced a dish known as "sauta thig." This, in all probability, was the first recorded blueberry recipe of the New World.

The journals of Henry Rowe Schoolcraft, explorer, Indian agent, and authority on the customs of North American Indians, often mention the prevalence of widespread clons of "whortle berries" along the route of his explorations, and the uses to which the Indians put them. In 1831, in an entry reporting on his explorations of the Namakagon, a tributary of the St. Croix, which flows into the Mississippi at a point in northwestern Wisconsin, he wrote:

"Both banks of the river are literally covered with the ripe whortle berry — it is large and delicious. The Indians feast on it. Thousands and thousands of bushels of this fruit could be gathered with little labor. It is seen in the dried state at every lodge. All the careful Indian housewives dry it. It is used as a seasoning for soups."

In another passage he noted that some Indians he had found half starving had been living on nothing but "whortle berries" for weeks. Schoolcraft also observed Indians preparing wild duck in a kettle of boiling water, thickening the liquid with the berries.

The early Indians marked the beginning of summer by the appearance of blueberries. They gathered blueberries by raking the bushes with their fingers. In swamp areas they sometimes pushed their canoes close to shore and beat the bushes over the edges of their barks, stripping the berries into large baskets.

The Indians dried the berries, not only on rush mats, but in large open baskets placed in the sun. They often cooked dried blueberries with dried corn sweetened with maple syrup. Other combinations were dried berries with wild rice and venison, dried berries in a sweet bread or a kind of pudding, and dried berries used as a seasoning in soups. They pounded dried blueberries into meat and carried this, along with parched corn, maple sugar, and water on expeditions. In the northwestern part of our country, they smoke-dried blueberries in large quantities. There is even some evidence that they made some attempts to cultivate, for they practiced burning, apparently realizing that the bushes do not bear when overgrown with brush and weeds.

Many pioneer families in New England emulated the Indians, using the berries especially as a substitute for sugar which was scarce and expensive. They gathered the berries wild from the fertile fields, along with wild strawberries, blackberries, raspberries, grapes, and free-growing herbs, making delectable jellies and jams for their families and sometimes for trading and selling. The early Shaker members were noted for this.

The first settlers also used blueberries as medicine. Hunters and scouts often found these berries life savers when other foods became scarce, and many were the itinerant merchants who made a meal of this luscious fruit along a weary way.

For wild animals and birds, the blueberry has meant, and still often means, the continuance of life. Rodents, grouse, martens, coyotes, elk, and deer feed upon the berries or leaves. Grizzly bears and black bears come out of their forest hideaways onto the sunny slopes if need be to get their fill of blueberries. They follow the growth up the mountain paths, sometimes traveling for miles to find a succulent blueberry patch.

Although the blueberry in the wild was popular as a food from the time the Pilgrims settled here, little was done to cultivate the plant or to improve the quality of blueberries for nearly 300 years.

Then, in 1906, a man named Frederick V. Coville, a botanist in the service of the U.S. Department of Agriculture, began his experiments in the culture of the Highbush Blueberry in the wild, and in 1909 started a breeding program. The burgeoning blueberry business of today owes a great debt to this individual who laid the foundation for a new and increasingly important American industry. The large size of the blueberries you find in stores today may be attributed to the early experiments of Dr. Coville and other dedicated scientists who followed him to improve upon this wonder which nature had wrought. Such breeding has produced hardy, cultivated blueberries triple the size of the best wild blueberries.

In the years between 1906 and 1910, Dr. Coville discovered that the blueberry plant requires an acid soil. His experiments disclosed that many other plants, such as rhododendrons, azaleas, mountain laurel, and trailing arbutus similarly need soil that is acid. This was something that, surprisingly enough, horticulturists had not recognized until that time. Following this discovery, Dr. Coville devoted two years to the life history of the blueberry, then successfully grew berries from the seed of the fruit, and subsequently perfected ways of propagating selected plants.

On the basis of Dr. Coville's breeding experiments, wild plants with superior fruit were sought for breeding purposes. The first such plant selected was the *Brooks,* a Highbush Blueberry, named after the owner of the pasture at Greenfield, New Hampshire, in which the plant was found in July, 1908. According to Dr. Coville's account, it took three summers of cursory observation in the mountains of southern New Hampshire, and three weeks of diligent search during the summer of 1908, to find this ideal bush which grew at an elevation of 950 feet above the sea. It stood with many other blueberry plants in an old, brushy, mountain pasture, rooted in acid and permanently moist, but not swampy, soil. This one bush alone bore the size and type of fruit the scientist was seeking. He regarded its selection as of fundamental importance to the success of his blueberry breeding experiments.

Subsequently, Dr. Coville discovered the *Russell,* a Lowbush Blueberry, on another mountain farm in Greenfield, and began a cross-pollination program which resulted in the production of about 3,000 hybrid plants which grew to maturity in the fields with remarkably successful results.

In 1910 Dr. Coville issued a modest-sized brochure entitled, "Experiments in Blueberry Culture," which reported upon his efforts to domesticate the wild berry and predicted that an agricultural crop could be developed that would benefit the whole country. The bulletin came to the attention of Miss Elizabeth C. White of Whitesbog, New Jersey, who, with her father, cultivated and marketed cranberries. (Cranberries are closely related generically to the blueberry.) The Whites had many choice wild bushes on their land which grew around the margins of their cranberry bogs.

Elizabeth White had long yearned for the development of a large, juicy blueberry which could be marketed as were her cranberries. Upon reading Dr. Coville's report she immediately got in touch with him, proposing a cooperative project through which Dr. Coville's research findings could be applied to practical blueberry culture. Her proposal was accepted and a long and agreeable association began. Tedious, painstaking, and unceasing though the work must have been at times, it was also rewarding, according to the accounts of both.

Finding the right plants for breeding experiments became an exhausting job, often full of adventure. At one time Dr. Coville and Miss White issued a kind of "Wanted" bulletin through which they offered rewards of $25 to $50 to anyone who could supply them with desirable plants. They sought to enlist the help of wild-blueberry pickers in New Jersey, and through this source on July 20, 1911, Dr. Coville discovered a third and highly important selection—the *Sooy.*

"I stopped at the house of Ezekiel Sooy, an experienced picker of wild blueberries, living in Browns Mills," Dr. Coville wrote in one of his reports. "It had been stipulated that a wild blueberry, to be valuable, must be half an inch in diameter. Mr. Sooy said that he hadn't any half-inch berries for me, that all the good bushes had berries *much larger than that!*

"He proceeded to take me to one of them . . . The berry proved to be a beauty, five-eighths of an inch in diameter. I started to arrange that a portion of the bush be taken up later when the plant was dormant, but Mr. Sooy took hold of a rooted sucker about an inch in diameter and ripped it from the ground with a forceful yank."

Dr. Coville was understandably shocked at this for he habitually took great care to transplant the plants he selected in the proper season and in the most delicate manner. When he protested, however, Mr. Sooy assured him that the root would grow, saying:

"You *can't* kill a blueberry bush!"

The top was cut off and the root wrapped in a wet newspaper. It was then taken to Washington, D.C. where, under the name Sooy, it did indeed grow to become one of the progenitors of some of our best blueberry hybrids.

By breeding and crossbreeding, by improving methods of propagating and caring for blueberries, by bringing the advantages of the blueberry culture to the attention of farmers in all of the favorable growing areas, Dr. Coville and other early pioneers in this field eventually created the cultivated blueberry industry as we know it today. Coville's breeding work continued until 1936 during which time he introduced 15 varieties of blueberries, the first in 1921, the last in 1936. When he died in 1937, he left many thousands of seedlings and crossed seeds, and from these, in 1939, three additional selections were introduced. These 18 varieties have given rise to practically all of the superior bushes now under cultivation.

The continuation of Dr. Coville's work was assumed by Dr. George M. Darrow of the U.S. Department of Agriculture, in Beltsville, Maryland. Although retired now, this grand old man remains active in the blueberry program, being perhaps *the* outstanding authority in the world today on this fascinating plant.

Many other prominent scientists have contributed to the development of this growing industry, their names too numerous to mention here.

Coville

The U.S. Department of Agriculture has cooperated through the years with state experimental stations in various developments of the blueberry.

Canning wild blueberries for commercial use began in Cherryfield, Maine, as early as 1866, and grew into an important business. Packing both wild and cultivated berries, especially for pie mixes, is still an important part of this branch of the industry, but frozen packaging seems to be outdistancing the canned in consumer popularity at present. We shall talk more about canning and freezing in subsequent sections of this book.

The first commercial shipments of cultivated blueberries were made in 1916. The industry has snowballed since then, and with thousands of acres under cultivation the value of such crops in some single states such as New Jersey, Michigan, and North Carolina, may be figured in the millions. Even states to the far south, such as Florida and Georgia, have successfully cultivated the blueberry. Thanks to M. A. Sapp, who in 1893 first attempted commercial plantings of the Rabbiteye Blueberry, a wild blueberry of the south, this variety has proven profitable in an area generally unfitted for cultivation of the Highbush Blueberry.

In 1950, the U.S. Department of Agriculture and the Georgia Coastal Plain Experimental Station began to cooperate in a breeding program of the first Rabbiteye varieties which has greatly stimulated the industry in the south. In Georgia, as recently as 1971, the Georgia Blueberry Association was formed, dedicated to giving the state a new major money crop —the blueberry.

The wild Lowbush Blueberry—in Maine, for example—continues to contribute to this growing industry along with the cultivated blueberry.

Blueberry Culture

Although many people, even the merchants who sell them, use the words "blueberry" and "huckleberry" interchangeably, the berries are not the same. One way to tell them apart is by examining the seeds. Blueberry fruits have four or five cells containing up to 65 very small, soft, inconspicuous seeds of which the diner may be unaware. Huckleberry fruits have 10 cells and about 10 large bony seeds per berry, each surrounded by a hard covering, which are inclined to stick between the teeth and crack loudly when eaten (which explains their frequently used nickname, "crack-erberry").

In general, blueberries are a brighter blue and have a slightly frosted look while huckleberries are darker, purplish—almost black—although there are "black" blueberries, and blue huckleberries too. Huckleberry leaves are dotted on the underside with resinous spots not found on blueberry leaves. You will seldom find huckleberries sold in the market because the plants are not productive like the blueberries.

I've ceased trying to argue about the incorrect labeling of the tiny, softer-seeded blueberry as a "huckleberry." Suffice it to say that east of the Appalachians we usually call our small-seeded plants "blueberries." Further west, they grow "huckleberries." By whatever name, they are delightful.

There is something quite exciting about picking your own bucket of blueberries to be used in a short time as a breakfast treat, or in a supper dessert. Robert Frost has sung about it in his poetry. Andrew Wyeth has immortalized the experience in his paintings.

"Going blueberrying" is one of the delights of childhood that lasts into full maturity. It's fun until you're 90! Blueberrying takes one out into the open air and close to the natural world. It acquaints one with all of the elemental earth smells that make up so much a part of memory. It provides opportunity for endless small discoveries — a particular joy to children. There is an ever-present anticipation of quick reward, and a feeling of accomplishment after a short period of effort. Not to be dismissed lightly is the good feeling of having easily and happily contributed to the family larder.

There are over 50 species of blueberries. None are poisonous, although not all are very edible. Learning the various names in English, let alone Latin, for all of the blueberry species is a little like memorizing all of the bones in the human body. Unless you're going to go into the blueberry business it is not necessary either. However, being able to recognize the more common types that grow wild, particularly those in your own area, and being able to look forward to the arrival of their various seasons, can provide much pleasure. If you become so enamoured of the blueberry that you'd like to grow your own in a cultivated patch, it is well to know something about those you can and cannot grow successfully, and to have a clear understanding of when and how to plant, care for, and reap this beautiful and delicious fruit.

If you want detailed information about blueberry varieties and culture, excellent aid is available through your state extension service of the U.S. Department of Agriculture. Other sources of help include state universities, particularly those of Maine, New Hampshire, New Jersey, Michigan and North Carolina. State Blueberry Growers Associations, individual growers and packers, and a variety of recent books on small fruit culture, available through libraries, are good sources of information, too.

In these pages I will discuss only a few of the more important varieties of blueberries, using the commonest known names, and mentioning some of the rudimentary things you might like to know about the blueberry industry. Wild or cultivated, the blueberry is a fruit to be enjoyed by all. It can be a lovely jewel in the good cook's treasury of priceless recipes.

VARIETIES OF BLUEBERRIES

Fruits from eight species of blueberries are harvested extensively in different parts of the United States, and fruits from three others to a limited extent. The types of primary economic significance are the *Lowbush, Highbush, Rabbiteye,* and after them, the *Dryland, Evergreen,* and *Mountain Blueberry.*

The Lowbush Blueberry. This most important commercial wild species is native to the northeastern United States west to Minnesota and adjacent to parts of Canada. This is the type which grows on "my hill" in New Hampshire.

The fruit from this species is gathered in commercial quantities from Maine to Minnesota, and southward in the Alleghenies to West Virginia. It is an upland plant, seldom more than 18 inches high, more frequently no more than 10 inches, which spreads slowly into large patches or "clons" by means of underground shoots. Some of these colonies of plants grow to vast sizes and last for centuries. The species crosses readily with the Highbush Blueberry. Its fruit, which is usually a strong blue, ripens earlier than that of the Highbush Blueberry, but the flavors are similar. There are early and late varieties of the plant. The early type, which is the common commercial wild blueberry of New England, ripens during July and August, the later one from July to September.

The wild Lowbush Blueberry grows more readily than the Highbush species in the New England states where winters are severe. This is because of the plant's low stature; the snow protects Lowbush plants from cold injury by completely covering them, whereas wind and cold can easily attack the exposed Highbush branches.

Most Lowbush plants grow wild and receive a minimum of care.

Nevertheless, the crop is extensive, and the earnings are important to the industry. The largest part of the crop is used for canning and freezing. The plant is easy to harvest by hand. In our home, we can gather all an average family will need for a day in just a few minutes of picking time.

It is difficult to visualize just how wild blueberry plants get their start. Probably the seeds are carried widely by birds and to some extent by animals. However they may start, in larger areas of the northern states the Lowbush Blueberry comes in naturally wherever the forest is cut or burned over. It is the custom in some areas, particularly in eastern Maine and Canada, to burn the fields every second or third year, thus killing back weeds and underbrush and at the same time pruning the blueberry plants. In addition, many farmers cut out or pull up weeds and brush in the fall previous to burning, or kill them with chemical sprays. Such methods do not seriously injure the blueberry plants if properly done during the dormant season. The berries from this wild bush are sweet and juicy, excellent for use in any of the recipes which follow in this book.

The Highbush Blueberry. This plant is the forerunner of most cultivated varieties of blueberries, important commercially to the fresh fruit market, but it also grows abundantly wild along the Atlantic Coast from northern Florida to southern Maine and west to southern Michigan. It is particularly prolific in western Massachusetts, Michigan, and the swamp areas of Connecticut, New Jersey, and North Carolina. The plant in the wild state is most commonly found on the coastal plains, but it is also present in the mountains.

This species of blueberry is a native of low wet grounds, bogs, swamps, moist rocky woods, thickets, and moist open fields at high elevations. It needs light and sandy acid soils in which to grow, with high organic matter content and abundant supplies of water.

The plant grows from 5 to 15 feet high, more often about 10 feet. The fruit ripens from July to August, but harvesting in the north sometimes goes into September.

Major commercial varieties include *Earliblue, Blueray, Bluecrop, Collins, Weymouth, Jersey, Berkeley, Late Blue, Rubel, Croatan* (N.C.), and *Coville*. New varieties, such as the *Bluetta* of 1972, are continually being introduced.

The Rabbiteye Blueberry. The Rabbiteye Blueberry is native to river valleys and the edges of woods in southern Georgia, southern Alabama, and northern Florida. Commercially, it is grown in these states and also in the Carolinas, Mississippi, and Louisiana. It is adaptable to a somewhat wider range of soil types than the Highbush plant and is quite resistant to some diseases which limit the cultivation of the Highbush berry in the South. It is not hardy enough, however, to adapt to colder climates. The fruit of the Rabbiteye is harvested from the wild to a very limited extent.

This bush grows to great height and size. Its fruit matures later in the season than the Highbush, the production of which is limited to northern markets at present.

Dryland Blueberry. This blueberry, also commonly called the "low blueberry," is native from Georgia and Alabama to Maine and westward to Michigan and Oklahoma. It grows only in the wild, being adaptable to dry, relatively poor soils of the ridges and hills. It is very drought resistant. The plant grows from one to three feet in height and spreads in colonies much as does the Lowbush Blueberry. Because it ripens later than either the Lowbush or the Highbush Blueberries it is sometimes called "the late berry."

The Western Evergreen Blueberry. Commonly known as "evergreen" or coast "huckleberry," this blueberry is native along the Pacific Coast from central California to British Columbia. It grows in open sandy woodlands and pinelands where there is partial shade. The fruit is gathered extensively in northern California, along the mid-coastal areas of Oregon and Washington, and in the Puget Sound district.

The plant is a many-branched shrub, normally from 8 to 10 feet high, but it may reach a height of 20 feet in open woods. The berries are usually small and shiny black, but may be slightly bluish, with a slight bloom. They have a characteristic strong flavor quite unlike that of other blueberries. The branches are important commercially for decorative purposes and are shipped by the carload to Eastern cities under the trade name "Evergreen Huckleberry." The plant ripens from August to November.

The Mountain Blueberry. This blueberry, also called "broadleaf blueberry," and more like the European bilberries, is a native of the high slopes of the Cascade Mountains of Oregon and Washington, and eastward to Wisconsin. It is most abundant near Crater Lake, Mount Hood, Mount Adams, and Mount Rainier, where thousands of tourists pick the fruit each year. It is very drought-resistant, matures its fruit in the late summer, even after three or four rainless months, and is important for forage.

Commercial Production of Blueberries

Cultivation of the blueberry is still in its infancy. Most cultivated varieties are the result of breeding and have been introduced only recently. They have been subjected to intensive commercial production and are very different from their wild ancestors. For one thing, dramatically increased size has developed through experimentation. Also, the latest commercial berries introduced have a particularly attractive bloom—a waxy covering on the skin—which helps give the blueberry a desirable light blue appearance and also prevents loss of moisture and shriveling.

Commercial blueberries are sold in many forms—fresh, frozen, canned, freeze-dried, and preserved—for use in an endless variety of food forms, ready-prepared for immediate eating, or packaged for future use. In normal years, with good weather conditions, fresh cultivated berries are available from the end of May until the middle of October. The first from the early varieties are picked about May 15 in North Carolina, June 15 in New Jersey, and July 10 in Michigan. The peak supply usually is available June 6 - June 23 in North Carolina; July 11 - 30 in New Jersey; and August 6 - 25 in Michigan.

New Jersey, Michigan, and North Carolina produce the greater amounts of cultivated blueberries, but there is limited acreage in some twenty other states. Maine is the leader in production of wild blueberries for commercial use.

A number of different varieties of cultivated blueberries are grown, selected on the basis of their different ripening dates, to provide the consumer with the longest fresh season possible. Research on the development of new varieties continues in the agricultural experimental stations of the blueberry producing states, in the universities, and on the farms.

Blueberry cultivation is a highly specialized business, requiring exact soil, moisture, and climatic conditions. Cultivation is not possible everywhere because blueberries need a very acid soil and a water table which comes fairly close to the surface and stays there. The best place for cultivation is an area where considerable organic matter has been deposited in ages past and which can be satisfactorily drained. The fields also need what is called air drainage, an open area not enclosed by trees or shrubs, to provide good air circulation. In addition, the plants seek a cold period long enough to permit them to lie dormant for a winter rest.

Plants for cultivation are selected on the basis of their quality and productivity. Hardwood cuttings four to five inches long are made while plants are dormant and are stored in a cool moist place until spring when they are planted. Usually, cuttings are rooted and grown for one year, either in ground beds in a shade house or in covered frames. The second year they are transferred to a nursery row.

After a year in the nursery row, they are called two-year plants. Well-grown two-year plants are then set out in the field, usually about 900 to 1,000 to the acre. This planting takes place as early in the spring as the soil becomes suitable for working. The plants may flower and bear fruit in their first season, but usually are not allowed to fruit until the second year. It is five or six years before a plant reaches its peak production. If you buy plants for a home garden, it is usually wise to choose three-year-old plants.

Approximately sixty days elapse between the time the flowers drop from the shrub until the berries ripen. Most berries are blue-black in appearance. After reaching their permanent color, the berries change little in size, but for several days they do continue to improve in sweetness and flavor.

When the berries mature each bush is picked about every seven days, four to seven times a season. Yields vary up to eight pints, or even eight quarts, per bush. Harvesting commercial plants begins when about one-third of the berries are blue. This is usually done by hand although mechanical berry-picking machines are increasingly coming into use.

Most of the crops in the major blueberry-cultivating states are marketed through cooperatives. These are associations which were organized to help farmers with their marketing problems and to produce the best crops by advising them on planting, cultivation, weed control, mulching, fertilizing, pruning, and disease and insect control. The rules set up in such cooperatives not only help the farmer but the consumer, for they regulate grading and packing standards, refrigerating and transportation conditions.

After the fresh blueberries are harvested they are cleaned by means of a winnower. Then they are cooled, sorted, and packed into pint boxes called "cups." In some areas, this packaging is done mechanically, in others by hand. Each pint box is covered with a cellophane or film cover bearing the seal of the cooperative.

Cooperative rules require that the container be firmly packed so that the berries will not settle, that they be of standard weight, that the berries be uniformly good from the top to the bottom, and that the berries in each box be uniform in appearance, clean, sound, and firm-ripe.

More than half the total cultivated blueberry crop is marketed fresh. Blueberries are packed in twelve-pint boxes to a flat wood crate, called a "tray," and moved to the market in refrigerator trucks. Customarily the berries reach consumers within about thirty-six hours after being picked.

The greater part of the blueberry crop that is not marketed fresh goes to freezing plants, though some is shipped to canneries and to producers of blueberry jellies and preserves. The processors pack under their own brand names. Canned blueberries reach consumers either in a syrup pack or as a "pie filling." Frozen berries reach consumers within a syrup pack or in a dry pack.

Buying and Storing Blueberries

Fresh Blueberries. Fresh blueberries may be bought from May through September in many states. The peak months are July and August. Early berries come from North Carolina and New Jersey, while later ones come from Michigan and New Jersey. The berries are generally highest in quality and lowest in price when in season. It is convenient to know that one pint of fresh blueberries yields from four to five servings.

When buying fresh blueberries, buy only sound fresh fruits. Look for clean, well-rounded, plump berries, purplish-blue in color, and pass over those which are shriveled, soft, sticky, or watery. (A whitish bloom is natural to ripe blueberries and is not undesirable.) Check the sides and bottom of the container for stains. These are often an indication of overripe or decaying berries. Check the weight of your berries. You should get a minimum of 14½ ounces of berries to the pint.

When you take your fresh blueberries home, do *not* wash them, but do spread them loosely in a shallow container so that air can circulate around them and the weight of the berries at the top does not crush those at the bottom. Refrigerate them at once for they are very perishable. If possible, don't keep them for more than a day or two after you bring them home. Ten days should be your absolute limit.

If washing seems necessary, wash the blueberries shortly before you are ready to use them, using ice cold water and handling them as little as possible. Drain immediately.

Frozen Blueberries. When buying these, always choose a firm, clean, cold package. Check for stains or water marks on the paper cover which may indicate a thawing and refreezing of the fruit.

Frozen berries may be kept in your freezer for up to twelve months without deterioration, provided the time elapsed between purchasing and storing was short. Once you have opened a package, eat soon after thawing. Leftovers may be cooked and kept a little longer.

A 10-ounce package of frozen blueberries yields two to three servings.

Canned Blueberries. It is sometimes convenient to buy commercially canned blueberries or canned blueberry pie filling for quick and easy meals. The canned pie fillings, already thickened, sweetened, and spiced, do save time. Can sizes vary, but the following is an estimate of the usual yield:

A 16- or 17-ounce can will provide about four servings if the liquid is served with the fruit, two or three servings, if the fruit is drained. A one-pound, 13-ounce can yields about seven servings if liquid is served with the fruit, four or five if the fruit is drained.

Store canned blueberries in a cool, dry place, and they will keep up to a year without losing quality. After opening, however, do not keep in the refrigerator for more than two to three days before using up, and keep tightly covered meanwhile.

Preserving Blueberries

By Freezing. Freezing blueberries is simple and easy, and a convenient way to assure the household of fresh fruit throughout the year. If quality berries, in proper containers, are frozen at the appropriate temperature, they will keep their natural color, fresh flavor, and nutritive value for many months.

There are three methods of freezing whole blueberries: *The Dry-Pack Method,* the *Syrup-Pack Method,* and the *Sugar-Pack Method.* In most cases the recipes in this book have been designed for fresh or dry-packed frozen fruit. Where you use syrup- or sugar-packed blueberries, you will, in most cases, need to decrease or omit the sugar used in the recipes. For detailed directions on how to freeze berries, see any general cook-book or write to your agricultural extension service.

I dry-pack most of my fruit because I find it easier to prepare for freezing (In fact, doing it is a breeze!), and because I can use these berries in cooking precisely as I do fresh fruit. It is true that most frozen fruits have a better flavor or color if syrup- or sugar-packed, but blueberries are the exception. Though I favor the dry-pack method, I always put up a few packs in syrup or sugar because these berries are convenient to serve un-cooked with milk or cream, over breakfast foods, custards, cake, etc. Not quite thawed, they make a deliciously refreshing dessert.

One important rule to follow in preserving your blueberries this way is to freeze them as soon after harvesting as possible. By doing this you

Hybrid

retain the berries' best flavor. If you plan to syrup-pack, you may find it helpful to make your syrup the day before you do your freezing so that it will be ready as soon as you have picked or purchased your fresh berries. Just cap and keep in the refrigerator.

Whatever the method you choose for freezing your berries, be sure to select blueberries that are fresh, firm, sound, full-flavored, about the same size, uniformly ripe, and preferably with tender skins.

For most of the recipes in this book you will find it unnecessary to completely thaw dry-packed blueberries. I suggest that you do the thawing in the refrigerator in the original container in order to retain color and flavor.

A word of caution! In using frozen berries in your recipes, particularly in baking, don't forget that they add more moisture to a recipe than fresh berries. Therefore, a certain allowance for this additional moisture should be made in preparing the dish.

By Canning. While freezing blueberries is simpler and certainly easier than canning them at home, many homemakers would rather can than freeze. The reason is obvious if there is no freezer, but there are other considerations. For instance, frozen berries simply are not as portable. If you want to take berries back to your home in the South from your home in the North as I do, it's pretty hard to keep the frozen berries as cold as they must be kept for a day or two while transporting them, but it's fairly easy to carry jars of canned berries in a container which can be kept at the correct temperature.

Then, too, we may be living in the Space Age, but there are still plenty of old-fashioned people who enjoy receiving and giving jars of homemade products on special occasions. (I can't imagine going over to Aunt Maggie's, or having her come over to see me, carrying as a hostess gift a package of commercially canned or frozen blueberries! But a home-canned jar wrapped in pretty paper? Yes, indeed!)

And — well — there's another reason. If you are one of the people who like to keep shelves filled with home-canned products for out-of-season use, they just would not seem complete without at least a few jars of luscious blueberries, especially if you live in blueberry country and have access to quantities of freshly-picked high-quality produce. At any rate, if you like to can, you may be sure that home-canned blueberries, when properly prepared, packed, and processed, will be every bit as nutritious as blueberries cooked normally for family consumption.

If you plan to can, pick your berries in the cool of the morning and do your canning on a cool day. Be sure the berries are flavorful, firm, ripe but not overripe, uniform in size, and without blemishes. Sort them out, remove stems, leaves, twigs, grime, etc.; then wash and drain them without delay. When you start, work quickly so that the berries will not be exposed unduly to air.

Since methods for canning blueberries are precisely the same as for canning other berries, I have not included directions here. They are easily available in most general cookbooks or through your agricultural extension service.

By Drying. Before the days of home canning and freezing the only method of preserving blueberries was by drying, a method fully utilized by Americans Indians and taught to our pioneer forefathers during our country's infancy.

Not too many people have the luck to own their own blueberry slopes as I do, but for those who do, and who have an excess beyond what they can use, sell, or give away, drying is one method of preserving them for future use. Since you will not easily find directions elsewhere, use the following:

Surplus berries can be dried in the sun or in the garret. They should be allowed to dry for 7 to 12 days to avoid decaying or molding. When done, they should feel dry on the outside, but should be slightly soft inside. They should be pliable to the touch, but you should not be able to squeeze water out of them. Don't let them get actually brittle.

There is no reason not to spread the berries on rush mats as the Indians did, but I would suggest spreading them thinly on trays, or better yet, frames covered with coarse wire netting or cheesecloth drawn taut to prevent birds from stealing them when dried in the sun. Unless you provide some protection, the birds undoubtedly will consider this opulence a

friendly invitation to come and feed. If you sun the berries during the day, bring them in to a warm room during the night.

When dried, pack in airtight plastic cartons. Before storing, remove contents of containers and pour back and forth on several successive days; by this means you evenly distribute any moist particles left among the dry ones and thus assure a more even condition of dryness. Store berries as you would raisins, and use accordingly.

Dried berries will keep for a year, and can be used in most recipes recorded in this book, if they are first combined with water to plump them. They can be used in almost any recipe which calls for raisins or currants, if you want to be innovative.

Blueberries for Health

We all know that fruit is one of the seven basic foods, and should be served in some form every day, preferably fresh and without sugar. You might be interested to know how the blueberry, which contributes such zest to the jaded roster of recommended fruits, stands up against others in terms of nutritional values.

Take one cup of raw blueberries and see what we have. First, what about *calories?* Your cup contains a modest 85, provided you eat the berries without additives, such as sugar.

Vitamins? Your cup will provide 140 units of vitamin A, .04 mg. of thiamin (vitamin B), .08 mg. of riboflavin, .6 mg. of niacin, and 20 mg. of ascorbic acid. (This last is enough to supply one-third of the daily vitamin C requirements for adults.)

Minerals? You have 21 mg. of calcium, 13 of phosphorus, 1.4 of iron, and 81 of potassium.

And the other *organic compounds?* There are 1 gram of protein, 1 gram of fat, and 21 grams of carbohydrate.

You may be surprised to learn that not only the fruit but also the leaves and twigs of this shrub possess medicinal properties which have been successfully extracted to treat abnormal functioning of the kidney tract and to reduce blood sugar. Our ancestors, who regularly depended on wild plants for home remedies in treating disease, often ate blueberries "to purify the blood and the liver." They believed such berries to be useful in cases of hemorrhage and stomach ache when taken in syrup form. Blueberries have also been mentioned by historians as a remedy for scurvy, a disease caused by lack of vitamin C.

As early as 1703 a book about Scotland mentioned that fluxes could be cured by "taking now and then a spoonful of the syrup of blew berries." To this day, some women in Russia concoct a preparation from blueberries called "chernika" to use for "stomache trouble." Anyone who has included blueberries in his diet on a regular basis will verify the fact that they act as an excellent laxative.

American Indians used blueberry juice and syrup to relieve tubercular coughs. It was a common practice among squaws to brew a form of aromatic blueberry tea to induce relaxation during labor. This custom, like many others originated by the Indians, was soon emulated by our pioneer mothers. Peter Smith's "Indian Doctor's Dispensary," (1813) described the procedure:

"Take a handful of fresh dry roots . . . take fresh tea every ten minutes until effective." The tea, the author explained, was believed to facilitate labor so that delivery would not be too slow, and would, furthermore, assure speedy and safe recovery. The tea was also used by Indian women to control excessive menstruation.

Despite all of these meritorious assets of blueberries, there is one type of person who should never eat blueberries or huckleberries in any quantity. This is anyone suffering from diverticulitis, for whom the tiny seeds of the berries wreak havoc when they pile up in the intestinal pockets which are characteristic of the condition.

Blueberries are highly perishable after harvesting, as are most berries. To retain their nutritive value, care must be taken in their handling and preparation. Immediate refrigeration after picking or purchase is necessary to keep enzyme action to a minimum. While the berries *can* be stored successfully for three to four weeks in a refrigerator, if picked when firm

and not overripe, it is wise to use them as soon as possible to prevent more enzyme action. Vitamins are easily destroyed if berries are allowed to become overripe. The longer-kept berries may look all right and may be perfectly safe to eat, but much of their flavor and food value will be lost. Be smart! Pick and purchase only what you can use immediately, or can or freeze without undue delay.

Always refrigerate your berries without washing or stemming. Do not destroy the bloom on fresh berries which is there to protect the dark skin. This waxy covering keeps berries dry and helps them maintain their firmness longer. Just remember that unnecessary handling causes bruises which bring about vitamin loss and increase enzyme action. Until frozen, don't place in air-tight containers either, or your blueberries will mold rapidly. Rather, cover containers loosely to allow air circulation.

When you are ready to use your berries, wash them quickly in cold water, handling lightly. Do not permit them to stand in water even for a few minutes, for this will result in loss of sugars and vitamins C and B. If berries must stand in the refrigerator for a while before serving, mixing with a little lemon juice will help to retard enzyme activity and aid in retaining the plump fresh look you want.

Since loss of vitamin C takes place rapidly when berries are thawed, frozen berries should be used as soon as possible after thawing. Cooking for the shortest time possible is recommended to avoid loss of vitamins.

...and how to serve them

Ivanhoe

All-time
Blueberry Blue Ribbon Prize Winners

INGREDIENTS

1 *wild blueberry field on a*
sunny slope
1 *bright summer sky with*
drifting clouds
2 *or more merry people carrying*
buckets (preferably children)
Dozens of fully-ripe
blueberry bushes
Multiple eager hands

NUMBER OF SERVINGS

As many as anyone can eat!

PROCEDURE

Look up at that sky and breathe deeply and let the sun kiss your cheeks. Now take the familiar "blueberry squat" or "bend" position and start picking. Put your hands down near the ground where the berries hang in fat secret sprays. Cup your fingers and rake upward so that you lose not a berry. Without further fuss or bother, toss those fresh berries into your mouth and chew.

You'll never in your life taste another blueberry dish as marvelous as this! But there are several runner-up prizewinners that may be yours when you've stopped sampling and seriously made an effort to fill your buckets.

SECOND PRIZE BLUEBERRY DISH

INGREDIENTS
1 bowlful of fresh, wild
blueberries newly-picked from
a fresh, clean field so that no
washing, but simply the
removal of bits of leaf and
twig is required.
Generous portions of thick
country cream
A little sugar, it you must.
NUMBER OF SERVINGS
One. Multiply by as
many as you want.
Any other recipes which appear
in the book are merely
RUNNERS-UP.

PROCEDURE
Don't be silly!

Breakfast Foods and Blueberries

Almost any unfruited breakfast food is delicious when topped or mixed with blueberries and served with sugar or honey, and milk or cream.

Try plain fresh berries with the cold cereals, such as corn flakes, shredded wheat, or Chex.

Try syrup-packed frozen blueberries, thawed, mixed in hot cereals such as oatmeal or cream of wheat.

Try fresh blueberries sprinkled with sugar and wheat germ or other health food preparations of the same type.

Prepare French Toast "from scratch" or use commercial product. Top with frozen berries which have been heated and flavored with a dash of cinnamon and/or nutmeg.

Make your own mixture of Granola, using dried blueberries instead of the usual raisins.

Muffins and Biscuits

BLUEBERRY MUFFINS

When I ask the men whom I know what their favorite blueberry dish is, they almost invariably reply, "Blueberry pie," but not so the women. Nine times out of ten their eyes will light up and their faces glow with nostalgic recall as they reply, "Oh, blueberry muffins, of course! The kind my mother (or grandmother) used to bake for me when I was a child!"

I think that the taste buds of most of us who were lucky enough to have had mothers or grandmothers who liked to bake are easily titillated by the sight and aroma of high-puffed golden-crowned, tender blueberry muffins served fresh and piping hot from the oven.

If your first sight of these gems came from an old-fashioned wood stove on a brisk autumn morning, you will always associate them with a delicious medley of other sights and smells too — the vision of a much-beloved gray-haired woman in a freshly-starched apron, a snowy white cloth in her hands, lifting the muffins onto a shining plate that has been carefully warmed; the sight of rich, creamy butter, home churned, patted into a cool dewy roll and stored in a thick crock, to be served up in elegance by a thick, scrolled, old-fashioned silver-hued butter knife; the delicious aromas of wood fire, and freshly-ground coffee brewing in a tall enameled pot on a stove . . .

Few of us have cooked or want to cook on wood stoves any more, despite the nostalgic warmth the memory of them evokes, but some of the recipes made famous through these stoves are still available, and the modern cook who has the time will find it an easy and enjoyable experience to produce home-cooked blueberry muffins for the delight of her family, even though some quite satisfactory semi-prepared mixes are on the market.

The following is one of the best basic recipes I have come across. Admittedly, it is "rich"; muffins can be made with less luxury. But who wants to surround blueberries with less than the best? The recipe was developed from a study of a number of oldtime family "receipts" and adapted to meet modern "hurry-up" standards. I hope that you will be your own gourmet cook. Try this basic recipe, then branch out and add your own touches, using the suggestions for changes which also follow, or your own substitutions.

Just one word of sage New England advice, though! Blueberry muffins *can* be made successfully with canned or frozen berries. Don't forget, however, that there's really no substitute for newly picked, sun-ripened berries fresh from the bush. (Particularly a New Hampshire bush!)

You may think that the quality of a muffin depends upon the ingredients that go into it. This is only partially true. The real secret in their successful baking lies mainly in the mixing of the batter. This is where a light touch is needed. Mix rather than stir, and do this gently by hand for no more than 15 seconds — just until the dry ingredients are moistened. The batter will look lumpy even before you add the berries. It should. A smooth batter will result in a tough, roughly textured muffin filled with holes and tunnels.

Two other steps are important if your muffins are to be baked and served successfully. First, be sure that you preheat your oven to the prescribed temperature. Why? Because you want your muffins to bake and rise evenly. Next, grease your muffin pans carefully so that when the time comes to remove the muffins you will not have to struggle with their sticking, and perhaps even breaking the muffins in the process. (Also, it makes the cleaning up chore much easier!)

It's been my experience that ungreased teflon-coated tins work beautifully for a few times, then I'm back to greasing again. But I'm not knocking them. You may be luckier. I just point out that where I'm concerned, they get their share of grease "just in case." I also like to flour the greased muffin cups lightly.

While butter undoubtedly lends a delightful flavor to the crust of a tender muffin, it tends to burn. Therefore vegetable shortening, rather than butter, is preferred by most cooks for greasing muffin cups. Grease well, not forgetting that rim at the top which sometimes catches an overflow of dough.

THE BASIC BLUEBERRY MUFFIN RECIPE

INGREDIENTS
1 cup fresh blueberries
2 cups sifted all-purpose flour
3 teaspoons double-acting
baking powder
½ teaspoon salt
⅓ cup granulated sugar
2 eggs, at room temperature
1 cup milk, at
room temperature
⅓ cup melted butter
OVEN TEMPERATURE
425°
BAKING TIME
25 minutes
NUMBER OF SERVINGS
12

Preheat oven to 425°. Grease muffin pan or pans. Stem, wash and drain berries; pat dry with paper towels. Sprinkle berries with small amount of sugar or flour and toss lightly to cover. (This is to prevent sinking in the batter.) Set berries aside. Sift and combine all dry ingredients in medium-sized bowl. In smaller bowl, beat eggs until light; add milk and melted butter. With spoon, make well in middle of dry ingredients. Quickly add the liquid ingredients, then mix lightly. Fold in the blueberries. Fill muffin pan cups two-thirds full of batter. Wipe off excess drops that may spill. If one or two cups cannot be used, fill these with water to prevent grease from burning.

Bake for 20 to 30 minutes. Test for doneness with wire cake tester. (Your Grandma used a broom straw, but we veto this for sanitary reasons!) Tester should come out clean. When done, remove from oven and let rest in pan for a moment or two. This will make the muffins easier to remove.

Serve at once on warmed dish covered with warm cloth, or in muffin warmer. If muffins cannot be served immediately, loosen with spatula and tip, leaving them in the pan. To reheat, put back into same muffin pan; heat quickly until hot.

ADAPTATIONS FOR THE CREATIVE COOK

The preceding recipe may be doubled or tripled, and extra muffins frozen and reheated.

The recipe may be halved, if only a few muffins for two or three people are desired.

The amount of blueberries in the recipe may be increased by half a cup.

Margarine may be substituted for butter in about the same proportions.

The amount of shortening may be increased to one-half cup and softened rather than melted. In such case, it may be creamed with the sugar, then combined with the egg and milk, or it may be cut into the dry ingredients, then the other liquid ingredients added. The result will be a richer product.

One egg may suffice, but two add richness and nourishment. So does the substitution of cream for milk.

Dry frozen blueberries may be substituted in the same amount for fresh blueberries. If these are used, defrost only long enough to separate berries before using. If sugar-frozen berries are used, sugar in the recipe should be eliminated. There's no reason dried blueberries couldn't be used in this recipe. In such case, plump them with a little water first, as you would with raisins.

For a sweeter muffin, cake flour may be substituted for bread flour, and the tops of muffins may be sprinkled with sugar just before popping them into the oven, or the amount of sugar may be increased to half a cup.

Pastry flour may be substituted for all-purpose flour.

Three-quarters of a cup of brown sugar may be substituted for the granulated sugar.

More salt may be added to meet your taste.

A teaspoonful of grated orange or lemon rind may be used in batter to add a piquant flavor.

Three-fourths of a cup of yellow cornmeal may be substituted for the same proportions of regular flour in the recipe. In such case, sugar the fresh blueberries before you add them to the batter.

ELLEN'S BLUEBERRY BISCUITS*

INGREDIENTS
1 cup fresh blueberries
3 heaping tablespoons
confectioner's sugar
2 cups all-purpose flour
3 teaspoons double-acting
baking powder
¾ teaspoon salt
½ cup cold butter or margarine
(or half butter, half lard)
⅔ cup cold milk (about)
OVEN TEMPERATURE
450°
BAKING TIME
12-14 minutes
NUMBER OF SERVINGS
6-7

Preheat oven to 450°. Wash, drain, and dry blueberries, then mix sugar into them to cover. Sift and measure flour. Resift with baking powder and salt. Cut butter into slices or chunks and add to the flour mixture; blend with pastry blender until butter is about the size of small peas. Add milk, stirring with a fork, until dough is soft and light and will hold together. Do not add so much milk that the dough will become sticky.

With floured hands, gently roll dough together into a ball and place on a lightly floured board or pastry sheet. Knead *just a little*. Roll to about one-half an inch thickness. Cut biscuits with medium-sized cutter dipped in flour. Place half the biscuit rounds on ungreased baking sheet. Spoon the sugared blueberries onto center of each of these, then cap each fruit-covered biscuit round with one of the remaining rounds. Brush tops of biscuits with milk.

Bake at 450° for 12-14 minutes, or until biscuits are lightly browned. Serve hot with butter.

*   For Blueberry Cream Biscuits, whip one cup heavy cream and substitute for shortening and milk in this recipe.

OLD-TIME BLUEBERRY DROP BISCUITS

INGREDIENTS
1 cup fresh blueberries
3 tablespoons granulated sugar
2 cups all-purpose flour
3 teaspoons double-acting
baking powder
¾ teaspoon salt
2 tablespoons shortening, cold
1 cup, cold milk (about)
OVEN TEMPERATURE
450°
BAKING TIME
10-12 minutes
NUMBER OF SERVINGS
8-10

Preheat oven to 450°. Butter a baking sheet. Wash, drain, and dry blueberries between paper towels. Mix berries with 2 tablespoons sugar to coat. Sift and measure flour. Resift with baking powder and salt. With pastry blender, cut the shortening into the dry ingredients. Add milk all at once, stirring with a fork. Add blueberries.

Drop by spoonfuls on baking sheet, about one inch apart. Sprinkle biscuits with remaining spoonful of sugar. Bake for about 12 minutes, or until biscuits are lightly browned. Serve hot with butter.

Pancakes, Waffles, and Fritters

BLUEBERRY PANCAKES

If it's true that blueberry pie usually gets the vote of the menfolk, and blueberry muffins that of the women, you may be sure that blueberry pancakes are the all-time favorite of the small fry.

My parents usually called them "griddlecakes," and their parents called them "stacks," or "flapjacks," but I had a great-uncle — a rugged old mountaineer who had spent some time working in lumber camps — who always referred to them as "flannel cakes." The modern and popular pancake houses have tended to make "pancake" the favored term. Whatever the name used, with blueberries they make a scrumptious treat, albeit, a fattening one.

Every spring I look forward to resumption of the Sunday "Pancakes on the Common" put on by one or another of our local businessmen's organizations in our little town of Whitefield, New Hampshire, to finance their charitable works. Blueberry pancakes are the feature, though baked beans, aromatic sausage cakes, real New England maple syrup, and steaming pots of coffee, plus other goodies, serve to intrigue the palates of "summer people" as well as native inhabitants.

I rather suspect that those pancakes come fresh from a store-bought package, but I never ask, and they always taste delicious, especially when there's still a bit of a zing in the air around our little bandstand, and the picnic tables are crowded with wool-mittened youngsters eagerly reaching for more, and teasing each other about which one got the most berries in his stack.

There's nothing at all wrong with the good packaged pancake preparations on the market today, but it's very easy and quite rewarding, too, to make one's own cakes "from scratch." Then you have an opportunity to try your creativity in making them "just a little bit better" than you've ever tasted them before. Cooked in a spider over an open fire in the woods beside a running brook, or elegantly prepared over a modern range in a luxury condominium, blueberry pancakes are prize winners among delectable foods.

Highbush

Here's a basic recipe that's easy to prepare and toothsome and has many propensities for adaptation.

BASIC PANCAKE RECIPE

INGREDIENTS
2 cups all-purpose flour
3 teaspoons double-acting
baking powder
2 tablespoons granulated sugar
¾ teaspoon salt
2 eggs, at room temperature
1½ cups sweet milk, at
room temperature
¼ cup melted butter or
margarine, cooled to room
temperature
BAKING TIME
About 10 minutes
NUMBER OF SERVINGS
About 18 pancakes

(I suggest using a wire whisk for mixing this recipe.)
Sift and measure flour. Resift and combine with all other dry ingredients in a medium-sized bowl or a wide-mouthed pitcher. In a second bowl, beat eggs just enough to blend yolks and whites; add milk, and mix. Pour liquid ingredients slowly into dry ingredients, blending as you go. (Don't overdo this blending; a few lumps left in the batter don't matter; in fact, some cooks believe it improves the batter!) Add melted butter, and swirl to blend.
Now spoon your batter to determine whether it is as thick or as thin as you wish. If too thin for your taste, add a little more flour; if too thick, slowly add a little more milk. Most people like their pancakes on the medium-to-thin side. The batter for thin pancakes is usually slightly thicker than heavy cream, if you need a guideline.

Allow batter to rest while you prepare the griddle. (Batter may be made the day before and stored in the refrigerator, but with such a long rest you may find that it has thickened somewhat, and you'll probably want to thin it with more milk.) Mix batter a little again just before cooking.

Bake on a hot, lightly-greased griddle or in a large iron skillet for best results. (I much prefer butter for this greasing.) If you use an electric grill or frypan, begin by setting the indicator at 375°. (You may have to raise it to 390°.) Test for readiness by trickling a few drops of water on the heated griddle. If the drops just sit there, your pan isn't hot enough. If they evaporate, it's too hot. If they "dance," the griddle is ready. (If you're the doubting kind, you may wish to test with a coin-sized pancake, instead. This last isn't really a bad idea since the first pancake doesn't always come out exactly as you desire.)

Ladle or pour the batter onto the griddle, making 3½-inch circles. (Each cake will require about 2 tablespoonfuls of batter.) Don't crowd cakes or they will be difficult to turn over.

Cook on each side until golden brown, turning only once. (This will take about 2½ minutes for the first side, a bit less for the second.) Pancake is ready to turn when bubbles begin to form in the center and the edges crinkle and turn slightly golden. (If you have difficulty in turning pancakes, you probably have not used enough butter on the griddle. In such case, loosen the edge of pancake with a spatula and lift with fingers, if necessary. Then, before making more cakes, add more grease to griddle.)

If you want to keep the finished stack hot while you cook the rest (You'll only be able to cook about three pancakes at a time on the average griddle), place the finished pancakes on an ovenproof platter and whisk into a warm (300°) oven while the others are cooking.

Be sure that individual plates for serving are warm.

You probably won't have a bite left of this recipe, but if you do, leftover batter may be stored in the refrigerator for use on the following day.

BLUEBERRIES FOR YOUR PANCAKES

Fresh, or dry-packed frozen blueberries, or drained canned berries may be used for pancakes. (I prefer the fresh ones, frozen only overnight, and put into the batter still frozen.) I've kept the directions for blueberries separated from those for the pancake batter because there are a number of ways to combine them, and tastes differ. Generally, for a recipe in the amount preceding, about two-thirds of a cupful of berries will be just about right.

Here are the three most popular ways to use blueberries with pancakes:

1. I like to ladle the pancakes onto the griddle and while they are still soft, dot with as many blueberries as each pancake will hold, turning in the normal way when the first side of the pancake is ready.

2. Some people like to fold the blueberries directly into the batter, before ladling onto the griddle. (If you do this, handle gently so as not to mash the berries.)

3. Others like to prepare plain pancakes, then serve with Blueberry Topping, Blueberry Syrup, Blueberry Hard Sauce, or a Blueberry Jam Filling. (See index for recipes which follow.)

ADAPTATIONS FOR THE CREATIVE COOK

Remember that pancakes may be served as a main dish for breakfast or supper, or — with embellishments — as a dessert. Also, keep in mind that your basic recipe may be halved, doubled, or tripled, according to needs. You may:

1. Substitute shortening or salad oil for butter or margarine.
2. Substitute one-half cup light cream for one-half cup milk in the basic recipe, *or* three-fourths cup heavy cream and three-fourths cup water for the milk in the basic recipe.
3. Substitute light brown sugar for granulated sugar.
4. Substitute granulated presifted flour for all-purpose flour, thus eliminating the need to sift.
5. Add wheat germ to the liquid ingredients in the recipe, then mix with the dry ingredients.
6. Decrease or increase the number of eggs in the basic recipe by one.
7. Make your pancakes *very* thin, fill with fresh sugared blueberries, roll, sprinkle with confectioner's sugar and a little lemon juice, add to each roll a dollop of whipped cream and three whole berries. (Serve this one for dessert.)
8. Make your pancakes *very* thin, roll with a filling of Maple Butter (See page 136), sprinkle with confectioner's sugar, and top with canned, sugared, fresh berries, or syrup-packed frozen berries.
9. Make your pancakes *very* thin and fill between layers with softened, sweetened cream cheese mixed with sweetened blueberries, and topped as in 8 above.
10. Substitute buckwheat, whole-wheat, corn meal, or other flours in whole or in part for the white flour in the basic recipe.
11. Substitute sour cream, buttermilk, cream cheese, cottage cheese, and other dairy products for milk in the basic recipe. (But remember that such substitutions require other changes in the basic recipe and you'll need to test them.)

WHAT TO SERVE WITH BLUEBERRY PANCAKES

1. Of course, *MAPLE SYRUP*, the real kind if you can get it, served warm.
2. Plenty of *FRESH BUTTER*. (I like cold, solid butter pats that I can watch melt on my cakes rather than the whipped kind. For me,

margarine and other substitutes are out, but you may prefer to limit the cholesterol intake.)

3. *SMALL GRILLED SAUSAGES* or *SAUSAGE CAKES.*

4. Strips of *CRISP BACON.*

5. Corn syrup, honey, molasses, or shaved maple sugar, also preferably served warm.

6. Maple butter. (This can be purchased in jars, or made at home.)

7. Orange Sauce. (See page 130.)

8. Brown sugar.

9. Confectioner's sugar.

10. Softened, sweetened cream cheese with canned or sugared fresh berries.

11. Sour cream sweetened with brown or granulated sugar.

12. Yogurt with sweetened blueberries.

13. Baked beans. (Particularly good in the out-of-doors.)

14. Orange juice. (The tart taste complements the sweetness of pancakes and syrup.)

BUTTERMILK PANCAKES

Many people prefer buttermilk to sweet pancakes. This is just one simple recipe similar to many you will find available in almost any American cookbook.

INGREDIENTS

1¾ cups all-purpose flour	Same as preceding basic recipe, *with*
2 tablespoons granulated sugar	*one exception,* i.e., when thinning
½ teaspoon salt	pancakes, be sure to use sour milk,
½ teaspoon baking soda	or a little more buttermilk, *not*
1 teaspoon baking powder	sweet milk.
2 eggs, at room temperature	
2 cups buttermilk	
2 tablespoons melted butter or	
margarine cooled to	
room temperature	

COOKING TIME
About 10 minutes
NUMBER OF SERVINGS
9-10

LESLIE'S SOUR CREAM PANCAKES

INGREDIENTS
1 cup blueberries, fresh or dry-packed frozen*
1⅓ cups all-purpose flour
½ teaspoon baking soda
1 teaspoon salt
1 tablespoon granulated sugar
¼ teaspoon nutmeg
1 egg, at room temperature
1 cup dairy sour cream
1 cup milk, at room temperature
COOKING TIME
About 15 minutes
NUMBER OF SERVINGS
About 18 three-inch pancakes

Grease griddle and start to heat as directed on page 38 for basic pancake recipe. Wash, drain, and dry blueberries between paper towels. Sift flour and measure. Resift with remaining dry ingredients. Combine egg, sour cream, and milk in a second bowl. Add liquid ingredients to dry ingredients all at once, stirring just enough to combine. (The batter will be thick.) Add blueberries, stirring just enough to mix in berries.

Drop by quarter-cupfuls onto hot greased griddle. Cook until surface is covered with bubbles, then turn and cook until other side is well browned. Serve with hot Blueberry Syrup. (See page 127.)

*   Canned blueberries, rinsed and well-drained, can be used but may make the batter blue, if that matters to you.

CHEESE SOUFFLÉ PANCAKES

INGREDIENTS
½ cup fresh or dry-packed frozen blueberries
¼ cup all-purpose flour
4 eggs, at room temperature
¾ cup creamed cottage cheese
¼ cup cream
¼ teaspoon salt
COOKING TIME
About 15 minutes
NUMBER OF SERVINGS
About 14

Wash, drain, and dry blueberries with paper towels if fresh berries are used; thaw, if frozen berries are used. Sift and measure flour. Beat egg yolks in medium bowl until light and pale yellow. In second bowl, beat egg whites until stiff, and set aside. Using electric mixer, if you have one, slowly blend into the egg yolks the flour, cottage cheese, cream, and salt. Fold in the whites of eggs.

Grease hot griddle or skillet with large lump of butter. Pour a large table-spoon of batter into skillet for each pancake. Scatter cakes with blueberries. Brown lightly and, when bubbles appear on surface, turn, frying slowly so cakes will cook through. Add more butter, if needed, before cooking second batch.

Serve with Blueberry Sauce (See page 129) or maple syrup, and with sausages or bacon.

The creative cook ought really to have one novelty pancake dish to serve when the others become too familiar to the family. I've chosen this one for inclusion here because it is different and is fun. It may be served at breakfast, but it makes a lovely dessert, and is a different idea for the oddly-timed "brunch."

There are literally dozens of ways of baking pancakes with various types of flours. Since recipes for these are readily available in almost any cookbook I am omitting all of them here, even my favorite buckwheat cakes, save for the following, which I have chosen because I think cornmeal goes especially well with blueberries, and with them and maple syrup represents our unique American taste.

CORN MEAL BLUEBERRY PANCAKES

INGREDIENTS
1 cup fresh blueberries
1 cup white cornmeal
½ cup all-purpose flour
1 tablespoon granulated sugar
1 teaspoon salt
1 teaspoon baking soda
2 eggs, at room temperature
2 cups buttermilk, at room temperature
1½ tablespoons melted butter, cooled to room temperature
COOKING TIME
10-15 minutes
NUMBER OF SERVINGS
10-12

Proceed as in basic pancake recipe, remembering to thin batter, if necessary, with sour, not sweet milk. Add blueberries according to your taste. (See page 39). Serve with maple syrup, sausages, or bacon.

BLUEBERRY WAFFLES

Everyone has his favorite recipe for waffles. Any of them can be combined with blueberries. (My granddaughter says waffles are just "fancied-up ruffled pancakes" — the same batter will do for either.) Just the same, here's one easy recipe you might like to try.

INGREDIENTS
½ cup fresh or dry-packed
frozen blueberries
1½ cups all-purpose flour
2 teaspoons double-acting
baking powder
1 tablespoon granulated sugar
½ teaspoon salt
3 eggs, at room temperature
1¼ cups of milk or
half-and-half,
4 tablespoons melted butter
or salad oil

COOKING TIME
About 4 minutes per waffle.

NUMBER OF SERVINGS
6

Wash, drain, and dry blueberries between paper towels, or defrost to separate, as necessary. Sift and measure flour. Resift flour with baking powder, sugar, and salt. Separate eggs. Beat egg yolks until lemon-colored and frothy. Add milk and melted butter to egg yolks, beating lightly to blend. Add liquid ingredients to dry ingredients and combine lightly. Beat egg whites, and fold into batter. Now fold in blueberries.

Heat waffle iron until indicator shows it is ready to use. (Unless it is new, it will not need greasing.) Pour one tablespoonful of batter into each section, close the lid, and leave closed until the steaming stops. Lift lid and take waffle out with a fork. If lid seems to resist, leave cover on a little longer. Waffle is done if puffed and lightly browned.

Serve with butter and maple syrup, or Blueberry Syrup. (See page 127).

BEN'S BLUEBERRY FRITTERS

INGREDIENTS
1 cup fresh or dry-packed
frozen blueberries
1 cup all-purpose flour
½ teaspoon salt
1¼ teaspoons double-acting
baking powder
2 eggs, at room temperature
⅓ cup milk, at
room temperature
2 teaspoons melted butter or
margarine, cooled to
room temperature
1 tablespoon lemon juice
6 tablespoons
confectioner's sugar
¼ teaspoon each of cinnamon
and nutmeg
1 cup or more
shortening for frying
FAT TEMPERATURE
360°-370°
COOKING TIME
About half an hour
NUMBER OF SERVINGS
12

Wash, drain, and dry fresh blueberries between paper towels; thaw to separate frozen ones. Sift and measure flour. In a large bowl, resift with salt and baking powder. In a smaller bowl, beat egg yolks lightly with one teaspoon water; add milk and butter. In third bowl, beat egg whites until stiff; fold into other liquid ingredients. Add liquid ingredients to dry ingredients, mixing gently until smooth. Sprinkle blueberries with lemon juice, 3 tablespoonfuls of the sugar, and the spices. Add berries to the batter, folding in gently. Chill for at least 20 minutes; longer is better.

Drop batter by spoonfuls, a few at a time, into straightedged kettle filled two-thirds full with shortening heated to 360°-370°. Fry, turning as necessary, until golden brown (from 2-5 minutes). Do not try to fry more than two fritters at a time, for best results. Drain on brown paper or layers of paper towel. Sprinkle with remaining confectioner's sugar.

Serve with maple syrup or one of the dessert sauces listed in index and described on following pages.

NOTE: Deep fat may be used again, if strained.

Breads

BLUEBERRY BREAD

A delightful way to make use of surplus berries is to bake them into bread. You can use fresh, frozen, or dried blueberries for this purpose.

Make a number of loaves at a time, and put some away in the freezer to serve to unexpected guests, or to take with you as "hostess gifts." These loaves, baked in one-time-use aluminum pans, wrapped in foil or pretty paper, make welcome Christmas and Thanksgiving gifts, for they keep beautifully for up to six months in your freezer, and are a welcome addition to the more routine cranberry, banana, and date-nut breads and heavy fruit cakes usually offered at these times. They are easily warmed up in the oven for serving at parties, and they make wonderful treats to serve at teatime.

Of course, when you make your first batch, you'll want to serve one loaf, warm and aromatic, to your family; the members will insist upon it!

Following are three of my favorite blueberry bread recipes. I always double these recipes (excepting the one called "Big Spread"), for I like to keep extra loaves on hand in my freezer. One word of caution, though! Be sure loaves are completely cool before wrapping and freezing. Use freezer paper and seal tightly. Of course, label and date.

KIMBALL HILL BLUEBERRY BREAD

INGREDIENTS
1 pint fresh or dry-packed
frozen blueberries
3 cups all-purpose flour
4 teaspoons double-acting
baking powder
1 teaspoon salt

Preheat oven to 350°. Grease *well* one loaf pan 9½" x 5½" x 3", or two 4" x 6" x 3" loaf pans. Lightly flour these pans.

Stem, wash, and drain fresh blueberries, pat dry with paper towels. Defrost to separate frozen berries.

1 cup granulated sugar, or
1 cup firmly-packed
light-brown sugar
2 eggs, at room temperature
1 cup milk, at
room temperature
⅓ cup melted butter or
margarine, cooled to
room temperature
OVEN TEMPERATURE
350°
BAKING TIME
One hour
NUMBER OF SERVINGS
10-12 (one large loaf)

Sprinkle with small amount of flour or sugar and toss lightly to cover berries. Set aside. Sift and combine all dry ingredients, excepting sugar, in large bowl. In smaller bowl, beat eggs and sugar together until smooth. Add milk and butter. Make "well" in center of dry ingredients. Pour in the liquid ingredients. Combine with a few swift strokes, just enough to moisten the dry ingredients. Lightly fold in the blue-berries so that they are distributed throughout the batter. Pour batter into loaf pan or pans, filling about one-half full.

Bake in 350° oven for one hour. Test with cake skewer. If tester does not come out clean, bake for additional 10 minutes or until golden brown. Cool on cake rack for 5-7 minutes before removing from pan.

Lowbush

"BIG SPREAD" BLUEBERRY NUT BREAD

This is one for the church supper-bazaar, or the family reunion, or the annual picnic. If there's any left over (and I bet there isn't!) don't worry; it freezes beautifully.

INGREDIENTS

3 quarts fresh or dry-packed frozen blueberries
8 pounds sifted all-purpose flour
4 pounds granulated sugar
¼ cup double-acting baking powder
4 teaspoons baking soda
8 teaspoons salt
2 cups shortening, at room temperature
8 eggs, at room temperature
1½ quarts orange juice, fresh or frozen
Grated rind of 3 oranges
1 pound chopped walnuts

OVEN TEMPERATURE
350°

BAKING TIME
One hour

NUMBER OF SERVINGS
7 dozen (about)

Preheat oven to 350°. Grease *well* three pans approximately 20" x 12" x 2" in size. Dust lightly with flour. Stem, wash, and drain fresh blueberries, and pat dry between paper towels, or thaw to separate frozen ones. Sprinkle berries with small amount of flour (to prevent sinking in batter). Set aside.

Sift and combine all dry ingredients in large bowl. (With this size recipe, I bring into play my turkey roaster, or a dishpan.) Cut in shortening until mixture is texture of coarse-ground flour. Beat eggs until they are light and creamy. Add orange juice to eggs. With spoon make "well" in center of dry ingredients; pour in eggs and orange juice, followed by grated orange rind. Combine liquid and dry ingredients just enough to moisten the dry ingredients. Fold in the walnuts so that they are distributed evenly throughout the batter. Then fold in the blueberries. Pour batter into pans, spreading evenly to all sides.

Bake for 55 minutes. Test with cake skewer. If tester does not come out clean, bake for an additional 5 minutes, or until top is golden brown. Cool on cake rack for 10 minutes before attempting to loosen, cut, or remove from the pans.

WALT'S FRUIT-NUT BREAD

INGREDIENTS
2 cups fresh or dry-packed
frozen blueberries
3 cups all-purpose flour
1 teaspoon salt
2 teaspoons double-acting
baking powder
2 teaspoons baking soda
½ cup shortening or margarine
1½ cups granulated sugar
3 eggs, at room temperature
¾ cup milk, at
room temperature
1 cup crushed,
drained pineapple
2 teaspoons grated lemon rind
1 cup chopped English
walnuts or pecans
OVEN TEMPERATURE
350°
BAKING TIME
40-50 minutes
NUMBER OF SERVINGS
About 20 (2 large loaves)

Preheat oven to 350°. Grease three 4"x 6" x 3" loaf pans, or two 9½" x 5½" x 3" loaf pans. Wash, drain, and dry fresh blueberries between paper towels, or thaw just to separate frozen ones. Toss berries in a small amount of flour to cover.
Sift and measure flour. Resift with salt, baking powder, and baking soda. Cream shortening and add sugar gradually, beating until light and fluffy. Beat eggs until frothy; then add milk. Turn into the shortening bowl and blend. Drain pineapple. Add pineapple and lemon rind to liquid ingredients. Stir the liquid ingredients into the dry ingredients, mixing until dry ingredients are completely moistened. Fold in blueberries and nuts. Pour dough into greased pans. Bake for 40 to 50 minutes. Test with cake skewer. If tester does not come out clean, bake for 10 minutes more, or until golden brown. Cool on cake rack for 5-6 minutes before removing from pans, and loaves will come out easier.

BLUEBERRY COFFEECAKE WITH SOUR CREAM

INGREDIENTS

½ cup fresh or dry-packed
frozen blueberries
⅔ cup brown sugar
¼ pound butter or margarine,
at room temperature
2 teaspoons cinnamon
½ cup shortening, at
room temperature
1 cup granulated sugar
3 eggs, at room temperature
1 teaspoon vanilla
2 cups all-purpose flour
1 teaspoon double-acting
baking powder
1 teaspoon soda
¼ teaspoon salt
2 cups sour cream
⅓ cup chopped pecans

OVEN TEMPERATURE
350°

BAKING TIME
45-55 minutes

NUMBER OF SERVINGS
8

Preheat oven to 350°. Grease a tube pan. Wash, drain, and dry fresh blueberries between paper towels, or thaw frozen ones just to separate.

Blend brown sugar, butter and cinnamon together, and set aside. Cream shortening and granulated sugar together. Add eggs, one at a time, beating well after each addition, until smooth and creamy. Add vanilla, mixing well. Sift flour and measure. Resift with baking powder, soda, and salt. Mix dry ingredients into liquid ingredients a little at a time, alternating with additions of sour cream, until all are mixed. Pour *half* the batter into pan. Sprinkle *half* the butter, brown sugar, and cinnamon mix over this. Gently layer the blueberries over this topping. Cover with the remaining batter. Mix remaining topping with pecans and sprinkle over top.

Bake for 45-55 minutes, or until done. Turn out of pan and cover with Maple Glaze, if desired. (See page 128). Serve warm, with butter.

RUTH'S BLUEBERRY COFFEECAKE

INGREDIENTS FOR CAKE

½ cup blueberries, fresh or
dry-packed frozen
¾ cup granulated sugar
⅓ cup butter or margarine,
at room temperature
1 egg, at room temperature
1 teaspoon vanilla
1½ cups all-purpose flour
1 teaspoon cinnamon
2 tablespoons double-acting
baking powder
¼ teaspoon salt
⅔ cup milk, at
room temperature

**OVEN TEMPERATURE
375°
BAKING TIME
25 minutes (approx.)
NUMBER OF SERVINGS
6**

Preheat oven to 375°. Wash, drain, dry, or defrost blueberries as needed. Grease a 9-inch square pan. Cream together butter and sugar until light and fluffy. Beat in egg and vanilla. Sift flour and measure. Resift with all other dry ingredients. Add dry ingredients by thirds to butter-egg mixture, alternating with milk additions. Beat between each addition. Fold in whole blueberries. Pour batter into pan. Cover with *Crumb Covering* made as follows:

INGREDIENTS FOR TOP

⅓ cup all-purpose flour
⅓ cup granulated sugar
⅓ cup soft butter
⅛ teaspoon each of
cinnamon and nutmeg

Sift all dry ingredients together. Work in butter with fingers to crumbly stage. Sprinkle over top of coffeecake.

Top with half cup of Blueberry Topping (See page 136) and slivered almonds, if desired.

Bake for 25 minutes, or until cake tester inserted comes out clean. Cool for 10 minutes before cutting. Serve warm.

BLUEBERRY KUCHEN

INGREDIENTS
4 cups fresh or dry-packed
frozen blueberries
1 cup, plus 2 teaspoons
all-purpose flour
¾ cup granulated sugar
½ teaspoon salt
¼ cup butter or margarine,
at room temperature
1 egg, at room temperature
1 teaspoon lemon juice
Dash of cinnamon
2 tablespoons confectioner's
sugar (about)
OVEN TEMPERATURE
425° for 10 minutes, reduced
to 350° for 30 minutes.
BAKING TIME
About 40 minutes
NUMBER OF SERVINGS
8

Preheat oven to 425°. Wash, drain blueberries, if necessary, or thaw enough to separate.
Sift and measure one cup flour. Resift with ½ cup sugar and salt, to blend. Cut in butter to a coarse texture. Beat egg and add, mixing thoroughly to blend. Form dough into ball.
Roll one-third of dough to size to line bottom of an ungreased 9-inch, springform cake pan. Fit remaining dough up the sides of the pan to a height of one inch, sealing to bottom crust at edges. Mix together blueberries, remaining sugar, 2 teaspoons flour, cinnamon, and lemon juice. Pour blueberry mixture into kuchen shell. Bake for 10 minutes at 425°, then reduce heat to 350°. Continue baking for 30 minutes. Cool. Remove sides from pan and transfer kuchen to serving dish. Dust with confectioner's sugar.
Serve warm, with real or artificial whipped cream.

Fruit Compotes and Salad

A WORD ABOUT FRUIT COMPOTES

To be technically correct, a fruit compote is a combination of fruits stewed or poached in syrup. Few of the following recipes refer to cooked fruit; therefore, they may be erroneously described as "compotes." Nevertheless, I have found that the word is applied so often to describe a medley of fresh fruits or a combination of fresh and cooked fruits that it is generally acceptable. You may prefer to call them "fruit cups."

Almost any of the dishes described here may be served hot if you prefer. In general, however, the serving of fresh combinations assures higher retention of valuable food vitamins and natural sugars.

A fruit compote may be a combination of almost any plump, firm, ripe fruits, depending for the most part upon the fruits available and the cook's imagination. The following are but a few suggestions for tasty combinations with blueberries.

BOY SCOUT BLUEBERRY COMPOTE

This is probably the simplest and cheapest fruit compote to be had. It is free for the picking, and was devised by Boy Scouts for eating in the wild. If you have access to wild berries, this is for you.

INGREDIENTS
Freshly picked wild blueberries,
washed only if gritty or dusty,
Freshly picked wild raspberries,
strawberries, or blackberries.
NUMBER OF SERVINGS
Any number; as many
as you can pick.

Mix, stew, if you like, adding a few crushed wild mint leaves and stirring before serving.

BROILED FRUIT MEDLEY

INGREDIENTS

1 cup fresh or dry-packed
frozen blueberries
4 bananas
4 canned peach halves
4 canned pear halves
¾ cup orange juice
¾ cup light brown sugar
4 tablespoons butter
1 tablespoon sweet wine
(optional)

OVEN TEMPERATURE
350°

COOKING TIME
10-12 minutes

NUMBER OF SERVINGS
4-6

Preheat oven to 350°. Grease a large glass baking dish with one teaspoon butter. Wash, drain, and dry blueberries, or thaw as needed. Peel bananas and slice in half lengthwise. Arrange banana slices with peach and pear halves (cut side up) on bottom of baking dish, alternating fruits. Spoon blueberries into cups of the fruit halves and sprinkle a few around the bananas. Pour orange juice around sides of fruits, covering bottom of dish. Sprinkle the whole with brown sugar. Dot with remaining butter. Bake for 10 minutes, then turn up to broil for a few seconds until very lightly "toasted."
Just before serving, add wine, if desired.
This is very good served with turkey, duck, or chicken.

BLUEBERRY - MELON MEDLEY I

INGREDIENTS

2 cups fresh blueberries
4 cantaloupes or 2 medium-
sized honeydew melons
4 medium bananas
2 cups fresh raspberries
2 tablespoons
confectioner's sugar
½ cup semi-sweet white wine
(optional)

NUMBER OF SERVINGS
8

Cut cantaloupes in halves, or honeydew melons in quarters. Seed. Slice off skins, if you wish. Wash and thoroughly drain berries. Slice bananas to bite-size rounds. Place banana slices and berries in bowl and mix; sprinkle with sugar; add wine; and toss lightly to mix. Chill melon slices and fruit medley thoroughly. When ready to serve, fill melon portions with the other mixed fruit. Top with lemon, pineapple, or blueberry sherbet (See page 118).
This is a large dish and best served as a luncheon entrée.

BLUEBERRY - MELON MEDLEY II

INGREDIENTS
½ a medium cantaloupe
½ cup cottage cheese
1 peach
½ cup blueberries
1 sprig of mint
NUMBER OF SERVINGS
One (Multiply by
number you wish)

Peel cantaloupe or not, as you wish. Seed. Peel and slice peach. Fill hollow of melon with cottage cheese topped with slices of peach and blueberries. Garnish with mint.
Serve very cold.

BLUEBERRY AMBROSIA

INGREDIENTS
1 cup fresh blueberries
3 oranges
2 bananas
½ cup shredded coconut
3 tablespoons
confectioner's sugar
¼ cup orange juice
¼ cup Cointreau or Triple Sec
(optional)
4-6 red maraschino cherries
Several sprigs of fresh mint
NUMBER OF SERVINGS
4-6

Wash, drain, and dry blueberries between paper towels. Shred coconut, if necessary. Section and seed oranges. Slice bananas into bite-sized pieces. Mix fruits in bowl; add coconut, sugar, and orange juice. Toss lightly. Chill.
When ready to serve, add liqueur, then spoon into sherbet glasses. Top each serving with small sprig of mint and single cherry.

KISS OF KIRSCH

INGREDIENTS

1 cup fresh blueberries
1 cup fresh pineapple chunks
2 oranges
1 cup seedless grapes
1 cup fresh strawberries
½ cup fresh, or drained canned cherries
3 tablespoons sugar
½ cup Kirsch

NUMBER OF SERVINGS
8

Cut pineapple chunks. Section oranges, removing seeds. Wash and thoroughly drain blueberries, cherries, grapes, drying on paper towels. Slice strawberries, if large. Put fruit in bowl. Sprinkle with sugar. Add Kirsch. Toss lightly to mix.

Serve as soon as thoroughly chilled, with an ice, if you wish.

Earliblue

BLUEBERRY SALAD PLATE

INGREDIENTS
(For each plate)
2 slices thinly sliced bread
1 heaping tablespoon softened
cream cheese
1 tablespoon Blueberry Jam
(See page 137)
1 or 2 large lettuce leaves, crisp
3 grapefruit sections
3 orange sections
6 or 7 melon balls (Mixed,
if possible, of cantaloupe,
honeydew, and watermelon)
1 small bunch of seedless grapes
A few slices of any other fruit
which may be in season,
as peaches
NUMBER OF SERVINGS
One. (This is a full luncheon
dish. Multiply by as many
persons as are to be served.)
The ingredients for the dressing
make one cupful.
INGREDIENTS FOR
DRESSING
½ cup honey
½ cup lemon or lime juice

Wash and crisp lettuce leaves. Spread one thin slice of bread with cottage cheese; spread the other with blueberry jam. Put together and form a sandwich. Trim edges from sandwich, then cut into triangular or finger-shaped sections. You'll get about four tea sandwiches from each large sandwich. Wrap in waxed or plastic paper and refrigerate while making the salad. Select a rather large, flat salad plate. Scoop out melon balls. Wash, pare, and seed, if necessary, then slice the fruits to be used. Arrange a lettuce cup on one side of the plate. Fill with the fresh fruits listed, excepting the blueberries. Arrange attractively. Sprinkle the whole with the blueberries. Garnish with a few mint leaves. Place tea sandwiches on plate beside salad. Serve salad with honey dressing, made by mixing the honey and lemon or lime juice.

NOTE: Instead of the cheese-jam tea sandwiches, you may prefer to serve slices of Blueberry Bread, spread with butter, or Blueberry Biscuits or Scones. (See recipes listed in index and described on other pages.)

Blueberry Soup

HOT BLUEBERRY SOUP

INGREDIENTS
1 quart fresh blueberries
1 cup Burgundy wine
⅓ cup granulated sugar
1 teaspoon grated lemon rind
1 teaspoon arrowroot
COOKING TIME
About 12 minutes
NUMBER OF SERVINGS
About 4

Wash blueberries, if necessary. Then, in a stainless steel saucepan, combine blueberries with two cups of cold water. Add the sugar, lemon rind, and Burgundy. Cook for 9 minutes. Pureé the fruit in your electric blender, or force it through a coarse sieve, and return to saucepan. Mix arrowroot in a small amount of water, and add to the blueberry pureé. Cook for three minutes more. (Do not boil.) Serve at once, with each serving topped with dollops of sour cream or yogurt.

COLD BLUEBERRY "BORSCHT"

INGREDIENTS
3 pints fresh blueberries
2 lemons
2 cups dairy sour cream
5 ozs. tupelo honey
2 sticks cinnamon
1 jigger of full-bodied red wine
COOKING TIME
20 minutes
NUMBER OF SERVINGS
About 4

Wash blueberries. Slice lemons very thin, with skins, in crosswise circles. Take out seeds. In a saucepan, combine all but one-quarter cup of the blueberries with a quart of water, the honey, cinnamon, and half the lemon slices. Do not cover. Heat to boiling point, then simmer for about 20 minutes. Pureé in your electric blender or force through a coarse sieve. Chill. When ready to serve, add the wine, then spoon on the sour cream. Float a slice or two of the remaining lemon slices and a handful of whole berries in each serving dish.

Bluecrop

Vegetables with Blueberries

SWEET POTATO - BLUEBERRY SCALLOP

INGREDIENTS
2 cups fresh blueberries
6 medium-sized sweet potatoes
1 teaspoon lemon juice
2 dashes each of cinnamon
and salt
½ cup light brown sugar
1 tablespoon grated lemon rind
¼ cup cold butter or margarine
¼ cup orange juice

OVEN TEMPERATURE
350°

BAKING TIME
1 hour

NUMBER OF SERVINGS
6-8

Wash, drain, and dry blueberries between paper towels. Refrigerate until needed. Pre-heat oven to 350°. Grease a 1½ quart ovenproof baking dish.

Cook sweet potatoes in a covered kettle in boiling water until almost done. (About 15 minutes.) Peel and cut potatoes into ½-inch slices. Layer one-half the potatoes in the baking dish. Mix lemon juice with blueberries. Spread half the berries over the potatoes in the dish. Sprinkle them with half the brown sugar and lemon rind. Give top a single dash of salt and one of cinnamon. Make another layer of the remaining potatoes. Cover with remaining blueberries. Sprinkle the top with remaining sugar, lemon rind, cinnamon, and salt. Dot the top with small bits of cold butter. Pour orange juice over the whole. Bake for one hour.

Especially good served with fowl.

RICE RING WITH BLUEBERRIES

INGREDIENTS

1½ cups fresh, sweet-packed frozen, or canned blueberries
1 cup white rice, uncooked
1 tablespoon melted butter
1 teaspoon salt
2½ cups milk, at room temperature
¼ cup granulated sugar
2 tablespoons cornstarch
1 teaspoon vanilla
1 teaspoon grated lemon rind
1 teaspoon lemon juice

COOKING TIME
About one hour

NUMBER OF SERVINGS
8

If fresh blueberries are used, wash, drain, and dry them between paper towels. Oil a ring mold about 1½ quarts in size.

Mix butter with rice. Bring two cups of cold water to a full boil in a large saucepan. Add salt to water. Stir the rice in very slowly. Cover pot, turn to simmering heat, and cook for 15 minutes. If rice becomes too dry, add ¼ cup more of boiling water. At end of 15 minutes, uncover pot and continue cooking for another 5 minutes, shaking the pan occasionally to aid in making the grains separate. Turn off the heat and let rice stand for another five minutes, until rice is dry and fluffy. Fluff the rice with a fork. You will use only two cups of cooked rice in this recipe. If you have more, put it aside. Now, combine the two cups of cooked rice with two cups of milk and the sugar in top of a double boiler, over hot water. Cook until hot. Mix cornstarch in the remaining half cup of milk. Stir cornstarch-milk mixture into the rice mixture, and cook for 15 minutes. Add vanilla and grated lemon rind and pour into the ring mold. Chill.

Sweeten blueberries, if you are using fresh ones. Sprinkle berries with lemon juice. Unmold rice on serving platter, when thoroughly chilled. Fill center of ring with blueberries.

SWEET POTATO - BLUEBERRY SOUFFLE

INGREDIENTS
¾ cup fresh blueberries
6 medium-sized sweet potatoes
½ cup granulated sugar
½ cup melted butter, cooled to
room temperature
4 large eggs, at room
temperature
1 teaspoon grated lemon rind
1 cup orange juice, at room
temperature
¼ teaspoon nutmeg
2 tablespoons rum
½ cup molasses
OVEN TEMPERATURE
350°
BAKING TIME
1 hour
NUMBER OF SERVINGS
6-8

Preheat oven to 350°. Wash, drain, and dry blueberries between paper towels. Toss in confectioner's sugar. Peel, then boil sweet potatoes. When done through, put them through a potato ricer, or mash with fork or wooden masher. Measure out 2 cupfuls of pulp.

Separate eggs. In an electric mixer, if possible, combine mashed potatoes with sugar, butter, the egg yolks, lemon rind, orange juice, and nutmeg, beating well. Whip the egg whites until stiff and forming peaks; fold them into the batter. Gently fold in the blueberries. Transfer to a greased souffle dish.

Bake for one hour, or until the souffle is well puffed.

Serve immediately, topped with a few whole blueberries soaked in rum.

Blueberry Pie

And so we come to blueberry pie — a man's choice, always! A truck-driver's favorite. A fisherman's delight. A construction worker's lunchbox "must." A little boy's schoolbox preference. A lumberman's "snack." A cowhand's breakfast. A Blue Plate "regular." A picnic expectation. An epicure's secret passion. And a woman's sure "come-on."

When little Nellie Forbush of "South Pacific" fame proclaimed in lilting melody that she was "as normal as Blueberry Pie," she knew very well that she had that sophisticated man she wanted halfway "to the table" already. Girl or pastry, what a beautiful, delicious, wholesome, dependable dish she described!

As American as the Fourth of July, the blueberry pie is offered where-ever our countrymen gather to eat. (My husband has even ordered it *and gotten it* in a Chinese restaurant, despite a lot of shaking of doubtful heads!) Whatever the American Restaurant Association may think of me for saying it, I just don't believe there's any comparison between a "store-bought" blueberry pie and a homemade one!

Along with the baking of apple pie — the other perennial Yankee favorite — the know-how for making a good one is not only in the home-maker's hands — it's in her genes! Priscilla Mullens probably made many for John Alden and Miles Standish. Molly Pitcher undoubtedly knew more about baking a blueberry pie than she did about loading a musket. Martha probably had one ready for George before he crossed the Delaware. And you can bet your last dollar that many a returning patriot of 1918 was welcomed back by a war-weary Yeomanette or a starry-eyed "Mom" with a blueberry pie at home in the oven.

So if you have any doubts about your own ability to bake a superb blueberry pie, put them away right now. You can do it. All you need are fresh ripe blueberries and your own special, native gift, plus maybe just a little nudge in the right direction.

If you've never baked a blueberry pie before, begin with one good, fool-proof basic recipe for the crust, and a similarly reliable basic recipe for the filling. Innovations are easy, once you get the knack. If you have a family recipe that's been handed down from mothers to daughters for generations, by all means use it. If you're not so fortunate, the one which follows is dependable, easy, and rewardingly delicious.

The following *Traditional Two-Crust Blueberry Pie* recipe describes what I consider the easiest, most fool-proof way to make a tender, rich, reliable two-crust pie. This recipe has never failed me, even when divided or multiplied at any altitude or in any season.

I'm sure that you are as aware as I that the way pie dough is handled has as much or more to do with the way the pie comes out as do the ingredients which go into it. For this reason I've included rather detailed suggestions for handling. But even when in a hurry and somewhat agitated, I have always managed to make quite an acceptable pie from this recipe. Of course, it can be enriched (I tried further on to suggest how), but do try the basic recipe *first*. It may be so satisfactory that you won't want to attempt any innovations. If yours is the kind of family, or you are the kind of cook who becomes bored with a recipe that is used too often, even if it is "the best," the adaptations I've included may meet your special needs.

Ivanhoe

TRADITIONAL TWO-CRUST BLUEBERRY PIE

INGREDIENTS
1 quart fresh blueberries
2 cups, plus 3 tablespoons,
all-purpose flour
1 full teaspoon salt
⅔ cup lard or shortening
6 tablespoons ice water
¾ cup, plus 1 teaspoon,
granulated sugar
Dash each of salt
and cinnamon
1 egg white
1½ teaspoons lemon juice
2 tablespoons chilled butter
OVEN TEMPERATURE
450° for 15 minutes,
then 350° for 30 minutes
BAKING TIME
About 45 minutes

Select a 9-inch pan. Sift 2 cups flour; re-measure. Resift with salt. Cut in the shortening with a pastry blender until mixture is coarse-grained. Sprinkle a little ice water over part of the mixture and toss with a fork, then gently push aside. Repeat until all parts of the dry mix are moistened, using a little less or a little more water as needed to hold the ingredients together. Handle as little as possible. Divide dough into two balls, that for the bottom crust being a little larger than the one for the top. Cover with plastic wrap and chill.

Now preheat the oven to 450°. Wash and drain blueberries thoroughly and pour them into a bowl. Add the 3 remaining tablespoons of flour, ¾ cup sugar, the dash of salt, and cinnamon. Mix all together. Let stand while you finish the crusts for the pie.

Lightly flour a pastry cloth and your rolling pin. (Use a glass pin filled with chipped ice and covered with a roller stocking for very best results.)

Roll the largest ball of dough first to a ⅛" thick circle about 10½ inches in diameter, at least 1½" larger than outer circumference of your pan. Be sure to roll from center of your ball outward in spoke fashion, always lifting your pin between strokes and starting at the center again. Cut edge of circle with a pastry wheel to even the cut.

When ready to transfer this crust to your pan, there are three ways in which it may be done: (1) fold pastry in half, lift it, laying the fold across the middle of the pan, then unfold it; (2) roll around your rolling pin, then unroll over the pan; or (3) turn pie pan over on the circle of dough, tuck hand beneath the pastry cloth and the pastry, and invert, placing the dough into position, and removing the cloth.

When lower crust is in position, brush the bottom lightly with a little egg white, and let stand in refrigerator while you roll out your upper crust in the same manner as you did the lower crust, just large enough to fit the top.

Pour berries into the pie shell. Sprinkle them with lemon juice and dot them with butter. Moisten edges of lower crust with a little water. Lift the upper crust off pastry cloth and place on the pie, bringing edges of both crusts together, either by folding the edge of the lower crust over the top and fluting, or by pressing the edges with the tines of a fork. Cut slits in the top crust, or prick through at intervals with a fork to allow steam to escape. (Some people prefer to puncture a hole in the top crust and insert a piece of macaroni to form a little pipe through which the steam may rise.)

Brush upper crust with a little beaten egg white or milk. Lightly dust with remaining sugar. Run a strip of aluminum foil around the edges to prevent them from browning too soon.

Bake at 450° for 15 minutes. Reduce heat to 350° and bake for 30 minutes more, or until the crust is golden brown.

Serve warm with ice cream or whipped cream; or cold, either plain, or with a piece of sharp yellow cheese.

ADAPTATIONS FOR THE CREATIVE COOK

The basic recipe may be doubled or tripled; extra pies may be frozen and reheated.

Dry-packed frozen blueberries may be used instead of fresh berries, as can drained canned berries. (In the latter case, use less sugar in the filling.)

Margarine may be substituted for butter, or lard or shortening substituted for either of these. (My grandmother swore by lard for her pie dough recipes! Her crusts were marvelously tasty and flaky.)

Grated lemon rind may be substituted for lemon juice in the filling mixture. So, too, can vanilla (not more than one teaspoonful, however.)

Cinnamon may be omitted, or nutmeg substituted, or mace added to the berries.

You can thicken the berries with 2 tablespoonfuls of cornstarch mixed with half a cup of water or fruit juice; with 2½ tablespoonfuls of quick-cooking tapioca; or you may prefer to use a little more flour for your thickening.

Brown sugar may be substituted for white granulated sugar, or the two may be used together in approximately the same proportions.

The amount of sugar in both crust and filling should be altered according to your own taste.

Likewise, salt may be omitted, or increased, according to taste.

An egg may be added to the pastry mix for additional richness.

Grated cheese may be cut into the pastry along with the shortening.

Butter may be substituted for egg white when brushing crusts to prevent sogginess.

Vents in the upper crust may be decorative — made with ends of spoons, tiny cookie cutters, and other innovative ways of piercing.

Half the pastry may be kept in the refrigerator for a second baking, and used in another pie, or for tarts or grunts.

*　　*　　*

Beyond these innovations for the two-crust pie, there are certain other ways of baking blueberry pie that are popular and enjoyable as a change. Lattice-work tops, deep-dish, one-crust recipes, fruit-coordinated fillings, and custard mixes add zing to pies. And there are, of course, a number of ways to make frozen or uncooked pies, meringue pies, and so on. Also, the busy cook sometimes likes to bake her pastries ahead of time and fill them at her convenience with separately prepared blueberry fillings.

In the following pages you will find samples of some of these.

LATTICE - TOPPED BLUEBERRY PIE

A lattice-topped blueberry pie permits the cook to see the rich, deeply-colored berries as they bubble. It enables the non-cook in the other room to savor the mouth-watering aroma of the baking pie to the full, while anticipating the promises its sweet-spicy fragrance evokes. Actually, there's nothing different about the *taste,* but there are those who don't think it's genuine blueberry pie unless the top is lattice-worked. It does take a little more effort and skill to devise the topping and, rightly or wrongly, a pie is often judged accordingly.

To make a lattice-topped pie, use your Traditional Two-Crust Blueberry Pie recipe (Page 65) for preparing your pastry and filling, but set your oven to 425° to bake for 40 to 45 minutes, or until the syrup boils with heavy bubbles which do not burst.

When ready to roll out your top crust, use a knife or pastry wheel and cut pastry strips a bit longer than the width of the pie tin you plan to use, and about one-half inch wide. These strips may be woven across the top of the pie and when complete, trimmed at the ends to fit the edge of bottom crust. (Do this loosely; do not stretch.) Moisten the ends of each strip and lightly pinch them to the lower crust. Now finish the edge of the pie with the tines of a fork, crimp, or flute the edges of the pie with your fingers.

If you're pushed for time, the effect of lattice-work may be achieved quickly by merely placing half the strips in one direction across the top of the pie, then placing the remaining half across them in such a direction as to form a diamond pattern. The strips will cook together and give much the same appearance as the more elaborate weaving.

ONE-CRUST PIE SHELL

You will find it handy to keep in the freezer a number of cooked or uncooked pie shells for hurry-up pie preparation. Dividing a two-crust recipe doesn't quite do, for there's the danger of coming out a little bit short. For this reason, I am including for your convenience this very good one-crust shell recipe which freezes nicely. If you wish to prepare more than one shell, just multiply by the number required.

INGREDIENTS

1¼ cups all-purpose flour
½ teaspoon salt
½ cup shortening
3 to 4 tablespoons ice water
OVEN TEMPERATURE
400°
BAKING TIME
20 minutes
NUMBER OF SHELLS
One

Preheat oven to 400°. Sift flour and measure. Resift with salt. Cut ¼ cup shortening into flour mix with a pastry blender until texture is coarse-grained. Add water a little at a time to the dry ingredients, tossing lightly with a fork. Use only enough water to hold materials together. Shape lightly into a ball, then roll to ¼-inch thickness. Cut half of the remaining shortening into small bits and scatter over half the dough. Fold one way, and then across the fold. Roll out again and scatter remaining shortening in bits over the dough and fold as before. Roll into a ball, wrap in waxed paper, and chill well.

When ready to use, roll on a lightly floured board to ⅛-inch thick circle, about one inch wider in diameter than your pie pan. Prick bottom with fork. Trim or flute edges. Bake for 20 minutes, or freezer wrap without baking.

CRUST - BASE DEEP DISH BLUEBERRY PIE

INGREDIENTS
1 quart fresh or dry-packed
frozen blueberries
Pastry for Traditional Two-
crust pie (See page 65)
Juice of half a lemon
2 eggs, at room temperature
1½ cups granulated sugar
3 tablespoons all-purpose flour
1 cup heavy cream
⅛ teaspoon salt
dash of nutmeg
OVEN TEMPERATURE
400° for 15 minutes, then
325° for 40 minutes
BAKING TIME
About 55 minutes in all
NUMBER OF SERVINGS
6-8

Preheat oven to 400°. Prepare pie pastry as described on page 65, rolling into single ball. Wash and drain berries and moisten with lemon juice. Line a 2-inch high, 9-inch wide oven-proof baking dish with your pie-crust pastry, covering sides as well as bottom.

Separate eggs. Brush inside of pie-lining with a little egg white. Re-frigerate. Beat remaining egg white and yolks together and set aside. Sift ½ cup sugar, the flour, and nutmeg over blueberries, gently mixing to cover them. Fill pastry-lined pan with the berry mixture. Now mix cream, remaining sugar and salt, then blend in the beaten eggs. Pour this mixture over the berries in the pastry shell. Bake at 400° for 15 minutes, then reduce temperature to 325° and bake for 40 minutes longer, until top is lightly browned. Serve chilled, with heavy cream if you like.

CRUST - TOPPED DEEP - DISH BLUEBERRY PIE

INGREDIENTS
2 pints fresh or dry-packed
frozen blueberries
1 cup granulated sugar
2 tablespoons flour
⅛ teaspoon salt
1 teaspoon grated lemon rind
1 tablespoon lemon juice
2 tablespoons butter or
margarine
Dash of cinnamon
pastry for one-crust pie
OVEN TEMPERATURE
400° for 10 minutes
then 325° for 30 minutes
BAKING TIME
About 40 minutes in all
NUMBER OF SERVINGS
6

Preheat oven to 400°. Select a round 9-inch baking dish with 2" edge, or an oblong one about 8"x6"x2". Wash, drain, and dry fresh blueberries between paper towels, or thaw frozen ones to separate. Make pastry according to directions on page 65. Roll pastry ⅛" thick, in shape of baking dish to be used, allowing for an overlap of about one inch all around. Set aside. Combine blueberries in a bowl with sugar, flour, salt, and lemon rind. Turn berries into baking pan, spreading evenly. Sprinkle with lemon juice, dot with butter, and touch with cinnamon. Cover with pastry, fluting the edges all around and cutting vents through the center to permit steam to escape.
Bake at 400° for 10 minutes, then reduce heat to 325° and bake for about 30 minutes longer, or until crust is lightly and uniformly browned.
Serve warm, with heavy cream or ice cream, or "as is."

FROZEN BLUEBERRY PIE

Some of us are lucky enough to have bucketfuls of blueberries close at hand during the summer months, sometimes many more than we can cook or eat before the blueberry season is over. What then to do?

Many of us, of course, can the surplus, and others freeze it for later winter use. One of the nicest things to do with frozen blueberries is to prepare pie fillings in such a way that blueberry pies may be made in the future "in the twinkling of an eye," to borrow an old but very convenient cliché.

The secret of freezing pie fillings lies in the use of tapioca, which enables one to prepare fruit for future use while berries are at their flavor peak. Tapioca adapts to the freezing process as no other thickening can, and has the added virtue of being colorless and tasteless, thus affecting the appearance and flavor of the fruit not at all.

As long as I'm doing it, I like to take a morning and prepare as many pie fillings as I have pie pans. That, in my house, means about six. But since you may want to make only one or two at a time, I've cut my recipe down to proportions for *one pie*. Just multiply the recipe by as many pie fillings as you feel like making at a time. Remember, those pie tins won't stay in the freezer for more than 24 hours before the contents are transferred to other packaging, so you don't have to wonder, "What will I use for pies if all my pans are in the freezer?"

INGREDIENTS
1 quart fresh blueberries
1 cup granulated sugar
¼ teaspoon salt
¼ cup quick-cooking tapioca
2 tablespoons lemon juice
OVEN TEMPERATURE
450°
BAKING TIME
About one hour
NUMBER OF SERVINGS
6-8

Pick over berries to remove stems, leaf bits, and, if necessary, wash, drain and dry. Stir together the sugar, salt, and tapioca, then pour over the blueberries. Sprinkle with lemon juice, mixing well.

Tear off a piece of heavy-duty aluminum foil about 18 inches long. (Or use several thicknesses of plastic wrap or freezer paper.) Place one end of the foil over a 9-inch pie pan, carefully lining it and letting the overlap hang over one edge. Fill the lined pan with the berry mixture, smoothing evenly over the pan. Turn back the extra length of wrapping *loosely* to cover the pan. Put in the freezer and leave until firmly frozen.

Remove the frozen pie filling in its wrappings from the pie pan. See that all edges of top foil or other wrap are firmly sealed over and around the pie filling, and return to freezer for storage. Now you have your pie tin back. Your frozen filling may be kept in the freezer for up to six months.

When ready to use, just prepare 9-inch pie crusts as described on previous page 65, set your oven to 450°, remove one of your frozen pie fillings from the freezer, unwrap it, and place in the bottom crust without unfreezing. Dot with a little butter, cover with top crust in usual manner, and pop into your oven. Bake until syrup boils with heavy bubbles that do not burst. (About one hour.)

BLUEBERRY APPLE PIE

INGREDIENTS FOR FILLING
1½ cups fresh blueberries
4 large tart apples
½ cup granulated sugar
¼ teaspoon salt
2 tablespoons flour
2 tablespoons butter
2 teaspoons lemon juice
2 tablespoons confectioner's sugar

OVEN TEMPERATURE
450° for 15 minutes, reduced to 350° for 30 or more minutes

BAKING TIME
45 to 55 minutes

NUMBER OF SERVINGS
6-8

INGREDIENTS FOR CRUSTS
See Traditional Two-Crust Blueberry Pie, page 65.

Preheat oven to 450°. Wash, drain, and pat blueberries dry between paper towels. Prepare pastry and roll according to directions on page 65. Line a 9-inch pie pan with pastry. Peel and core apples, and cut into eighths; spread over pie crust. Scatter blueberries over the apples. Sprinkle fruit with lemon juice. Combine granulated sugar, salt, flour, and sprinkle over the fruit. Dot with butter. Place top crust on pie.

Bake at 450° for 15 minutes; lower heat to 350° and continue baking for 30 minutes, or until crust is golden brown. Sprinkle top with confectioner's sugar before serving.

Serve warm or cold, with sharp cheese or heavy cream.

BLUEBERRY - PEACH PIE — COOKED

INGREDIENTS FOR CRUST
See recipe for Traditional Blueberry Pie, page 65

INGREDIENTS FOR FILLING
6-8 fresh peaches
1 cup fresh blueberries
2 tablespoons cornstarch
1 cup granulated sugar
2 tablespoons lemon juice
2 tablespoons butter, cold

Line a 9-inch pie pan with pastry, using Traditional Blueberry Pie recipe. Peel peaches and slice in large pieces. Wash, drain, and dry blueberries between paper towels. Place peach slices in pastry-lined pan. Scatter blueberries in and around the peaches. Mix cornstarch in quarter cup of water. When smooth, add the sugar, and blend. Pour over the fruit. Sprinkle fruit with lemon juice and dot with cold butter. Cover with top

OVEN TEMPERATURE
450°, *reduced after 10*
minutes to 300°
BAKING TIME
1 hour
NUMBER OF SERVINGS
6-8

crust; flute, and gash to let steam
escape.
Bake at 450° for about 10 minutes;
reduce heat to 300° and bake for
50 minutes.

BLUEBERRY-PEACH PIE — UNCOOKED

INGREDIENTS
FOR CRUST
½ cup graham cracker crumbs
1 tablespoon granulated sugar
Dash each of nutmeg
and cinnamon
2 tablespoons soft butter
INGREDIENTS
FOR FILLING
1 cup fresh or dry-packed
frozen blueberries
1 can peach halves
1 package instant butterscotch
or vanilla pudding
2 cups cold milk
2 teaspoons cornstarch
2 tablespoons granulated sugar
OVEN TEMPERATURE
300°
BAKING TIME
15 minutes for crust
NUMBER OF SERVINGS
6-8

Preheat oven to 300°. Butter a 9-inch
pie pan generously. Mix all ingredients
for pastry. Press on bottom and sides
of pie pan, using fingers for start,
then with bottom of another pie tin
of same size to give a smooth appearance. Bake for 15 minutes. Cool.
Wash, drain, and dry fresh blueberries
between paper towels, or defrost
frozen ones enough to separate. Put
in refrigerator. Drain peach halves,
retaining juice. Put peaches in refrigerator. Prepare instant pudding, using
milk, according to manufacturer's
directions. Pour immediately into
graham cracker shell, and return to
refrigerator. Measure one cup peach
juice. Mix with cornstarch and sugar,
stirring to smooth. Boil peach juice
mixture on stove until it thickens.
Cool. Take pudding-filled crust and
fruit from refrigerator. Lay peach
halves over the pudding to cover, with
cut sides up. Fill peach cups with
blueberries. Pour boiled glaze over the whole top. Return to refrigerator
until ready to serve. Serve with whipped topping on each portion.

BLUEBERRY MERINGUE PIE

INGREDIENTS
See recipe for One-Crust
Pie Shell, page 68
INGREDIENTS
FOR FILLING
3 cups fresh or dry-packed
frozen blueberries
1 cup granulated sugar
2 tablespoons flour
¼ teaspoon salt
1 tablespoon lemon juice
2 eggs, at room temperature
INGREDIENTS
FOR TOPPING
2 egg whites, at room
temperature
¼ teaspoon cream of tartar
3 tablespoons confectioner's
sugar
OVEN TEMPERATURE
350°
BAKING TIME
About 10 minutes
(for meringue)
45 minutes for pie shell
NUMBER OF SERVINGS
6-8

Make One-Crust Pie Shell according to directions on page 68. Wash and drain blueberries, if necessary. Pour blueberries into a saucepan. Beat egg yolks slightly, then add to them the remaining ingredients for filling. Mix with blueberries in the saucepan. Cook, stirring, until the mixture thickens. Take from heat and cool. Preheat oven to 350°. While filling is cooling, beat egg whites in electric mixer at medium speed until frothy. Add cream of tartar and continue to beat until egg whites stand in stiff, but not dry, peaks. Slowly beat in the sugar. Now pour blueberry filling into pie shell. Spread egg white mixture over top of filling (from edges to center), being sure that it is sealed at every point with the crust. Bake for 10 or more minutes, or until meringue topping is slightly browned. Cool in a warm place, away from drafts.

Tarts, Cobblers, Crisp, and Dumplings

BLUEBERRY TARTS

When preparing tarts, make pastry the day before rolling and baking, if possible. Chilling overnight in refrigerator makes the dough easier to handle. Remove from refrigerator about an hour before rolling. If recipes for either shells or filling are too large, you may cut in half. I recommend making the dozen shells while you are about it, however; those in excess of need may be frozen for later use—a great time-saver.

INGREDIENTS FOR
PASTRY
2½ cups all-purpose flour
3 teaspoons confectioner's sugar
1 teaspoon salt
1 cup shortening, at room temperature
6 tablespoons ice water (about)
INGREDIENTS FOR
FILLING
1 quart fresh blueberries
1 cup granulated sugar
2 tablespoons cornstarch
2 tablespoons brandy
INGREDIENTS FOR
GLAZE
See Blueberry Glaze, page 127
OVEN TEMPERATURE
400°
BAKING TIME
15 minutes or more

To make tart shells.
Preheat oven to 400°. Sift flour and measure. In a medium-sized bowl, resift with sugar and salt. Cut in shortening with a pastry blender until crumbs are size of small peas. Sprinkle ice water over the mixture, one table-spoonful at a time, each time tossing the dry ingredients reached by the water with a fork. Be sure to reach all the dry portions. Using your fingers as little as possible, lightly shape dough into a ball. Wrap in foil or plastic wrap and refrigerate to chill. When ready to prepare tart shells, take dough from refrigerator and divide lightly into 12 equal-sized balls. On lightly floured pastry cloth, roll out the balls to form circles about 5½ inches in size. Use small bowl or pastry cutter to shape. Shape the

(continued next page)

NUMBER OF SERVINGS
12

circles inside a dozen aluminum foil tart pans as you would for pie shells. Trim excess dough from edges with a knife, or flute as for pie. Prick dough generously to avoid bubbles in baking. Bake for approximately 15 minutes, or until shells are lightly browned. Remove to a wire rack to cool.

To make filling. Wash and drain blueberries. Heat one-quarter cup water in a saucepan with the sugar, then add blueberries. Simmer. Blend cornstarch with small amount of water and add to berries. Raise heat and bring to a boil. Cook for one minute. Cool. Add brandy. Pour filling into the tarts.

To make glaze. Follow directions for glaze on page 127. Pour over tarts. Refrigerate until ready to serve.

Serve as is, or with dollop of whipped cream on each tart.

BLUEBERRY CUSTARD TARTS

INGREDIENTS
FOR SHELLS
See Blueberry Tarts, page 75
1 egg white
INGREDIENTS
FOR FILLING
(Cut ingredients in half, if you want to make no more than 6 tarts.)
1 quart fresh blueberries
6 eggs at room temperature
1 quart milk, hot
⅔ cup honey
¼ teaspoon salt
1½ teaspoons vanilla
OVEN TEMPERATURE
450° for 10 minutes, then 300° for 40-50 minutes
BAKING TIME
About 1 hour
NUMBER OF SERVINGS
12

Prepare Blueberry Glaze (See page 127). Make shells, preparing as directed on page 68, *but do not bake* without filling. Brush insides of unbaked shells with slightly beaten egg white before adding the filling. Next, preheat oven to 450°. Beat eggs thoroughly. Scald milk. Stir honey, salt, milk, and vanilla into the eggs. Pour mixture into the unbaked tart shells. Bake at 450° for 10 minutes. Reduce heat to 300°, and bake for 40-50 minutes, until custard is firm. Remove from oven and cool. Divide blueberries evenly over custard in tart shells. Spoon glaze over berries.

NEW HAMPSHIRE BLUEBERRY SLUMP

INGREDIENTS
3 cups fresh blueberries
1¼ cups granulated sugar
¼ cup flour
⅛ teaspoon salt
1 tablespoon lemon juice
1 tablespoon butter or
margarine
Dough for 1-crust, 9-inch pie
(See page 68)
OVEN TEMPERATURE
450°
BAKING TIME
12 minutes
NUMBER OF SERVINGS
6-8

Prepare dough for 1-crust pie as described on page 68. Store in refrigerator in ball shape until needed. Preheat oven to 450°.
Wash and drain berries. Combine berries, sugar, flour, salt, and lemon juice. Pour into a 9-inch square pan. Dot with butter. Roll pastry one-half inch thick in shape of the pan. Cut three small diamond-shaped holes in the pastry with a sharp knife or tiny diamond-shaped cutter (from bridge cookie set). Place the pastry on top of berries. Bake for about 12 minutes, or until nicely browned.
Serve warm with thick cream, sugared sour cream, or ice cream.

NEW ENGLAND BLUEBERRY GRUNT

INGREDIENTS
1 quart fresh or dry-packed
frozen blueberries
1 teaspoon lemon juice
2 tablespoons butter, cold
1 cup all-purpose flour
1 teaspoon baking powder
½ teaspoon salt
¾ cup granulated sugar
1 egg, at room temperature
½ cup milk, at room
temperature
Dash of nutmeg
COOKING TIME
About 25 minutes
NUMBER OF SERVINGS
About 6

Wash and drain blueberries, if necessary. In a saucepan combine the berries, sugar, and lemon juice with ¼ cup of water; bring to a boil. Immediately lower heat and simmer for 4 to 8 minutes while mixture thickens. Pour berry mixture into shallow ovenproof baking dish, one which has a lid. Dot with butter. Sift flour. Resift with baking powder, salt, and sugar. Beat the egg thoroughly. Add milk to egg, then mix into the dry ingredients. Spoon on top of the hot berries. Cover the dish and simmer for about 15 minutes until dough begins to lightly brown and berries are bubbly. Sprinkle a little grated nutmeg over the top. Serve hot with chilled, heavy cream.

YANKEE BLUEBERRY GRUNT

INGREDIENTS
2 cups fresh blueberries
2 cups all-purpose flour
½ teaspoon salt
3 teaspoons double-acting
baking powder
1 cup heavy cream, cold
2-3 tablespoons granulated
sugar
⅛ teaspoon allspice
COOKING TIME
One hour and a quarter
NUMBER OF SERVINGS
4-6

About one hour before starting, put bowl and beaters for whipped cream in refrigerator to chill. Wash and drain blueberries.

Sift flour and measure. In a medium-sized bowl, resift flour with baking powder and salt. Whip cream in chilled bowl with chilled beaters until it stands in peaks. Gently combine whipped cream and flour mixture, blending with a fork. Turn out on a floured board or pastry cloth. Knead for one minute. Lightly roll dough to ¾-inch thickness. Cut circlets with small biscuit cutter.

In a stainless steel or enamel saucepan, cook the blueberries, sugar, and allspice with ½ cup water until the berries are soft. Place berries in 1½-quart, deep, ovenproof baking dish. Cover with circlets of dough, placed close together. Set the baking dish in a kettle of boiling water, with water reaching about two-thirds up the sides of the baking dish. Cover kettle and simmer for 1¼ hours, adding water as needed. Uncover, and serve warm with heavy cream, ice cream, or Spice Sauce (See page 130).

BLUEBERRY PANDOWDY

INGREDIENTS

2 cups fresh or dry-packed
frozen blueberries
1½ cups all-purpose flour
¼ teaspoon salt
½ cup butter or margarine,
cold
½ cup granulated sugar
½ teaspoon cinnamon
¼ teaspoon nutmeg
½ cup maple syrup
½ cup butter or margarine,
melted

OVEN TEMPERATURE

400° for 10 minutes, lowered
to 350° for 50 minutes

BAKING TIME

One hour

NUMBER OF SERVINGS

6

Preheat oven to 400°. Sift and measure flour. Resift with salt in medium-sized bowl. Blend in cold butter with a pastry blender until mixture is texture of fine grain. Sprinkle with a few drops of ice water to hold dough together.

Roll the pastry out, brush with soft butter, and cut in half. Roll two pieces together again, and brush with melted butter, then again cut in half. This time use one portion to line a deep 1½ quart baking dish. The other half will be used later. Refrigerate both pieces, while you prepare remainder of pandowdy.

Mix together sugar and spices. Wash, drain, and dry blueberries between paper towels, or defrost just enough to separate berries, as necessary. Mix berries with the sugar and spices. Pour into the pastry-lined dish. Combine maple syrup with remaining melted butter and ¼ cup lukewarm water. Pour over the berries. Cover with the piece of pastry you set aside. (Roll it out more, if necessary, so that it will fit snugly.) Seal it all around, but do *not* prick the crust.

Place in preheated oven at 400° for 10 minutes. Take dish out of oven and cut the top crust into the berries, breaking into small pieces. Reduce heat to 350° and return dish to oven. Bake for 50 minutes or more. Serve with Hard Sauce (See page 132), or ice cream.

QUICK BLUEBERRY COBBLERS

(1. With Muffin Mix)

INGREDIENTS
1 large can blueberry pie filling
1 teaspoon lemon juice
½ teaspoon cinnamon or
nutmeg
1 package muffin mix
(corn is good)
2 tablespoons granulated sugar
½ cup milk, at room
temperature
1 egg, at room temperature
2 tablespoons melted butter
OVEN TEMPERATURE
400°
BAKING TIME
25-30 minutes
NUMBER OF SERVINGS
6-8

Preheat oven to 400°. In a saucepan, mix together blueberries, lemon juice, spice, and one-half cup of water. Bring to a boil, then take from stove immediately. Pour into an ovenproof baking dish about 1½-quart capacity. Combine prepared mix with sugar, egg, and milk, following directions on package. Stir until just blended. Spoon-drop over berries. Dribble melted butter over the topping.

Bake for 25-30 minutes, until topping is cooked through and lightly browned. Serve hot with cream, commercial sour cream, or commercial whipped topping. (This, of course, is for *quick* preparation; if you have time enough you may prefer whipped cream, gingered and sweetened sour cream, or one of the dessert sauces listed in the index and described on following pages.)

(2. With Biscuit Mix)

INGREDIENTS
1 large can blueberries
1 teaspoon lemon juice
1 to 3 tablespoons granulated
sugar (to taste)
1 cup biscuit mix
1 tablespoon cornstarch
2 tablespoons butter or
margarine, cold
½ teaspoon cinnamon or
nutmeg
¼ cup plus 2 tablespoons
cream

Preheat oven to 400°. In a stainless steel or enamel saucepan, heat blueberries. Add lemon juice and sugar to taste. Dissolve cornstarch in 2 tablespoons cold water and add to berries, stirring to blend. Boil for one minute. Pour into a 1½-quart, round, ovenproof baking casserole or dish. Dot with butter, and sprinkle with spice.

Mix biscuit mix with about 1 table-spoonful of sugar and the cream, using a fork to blend. Beat with fork for

OVEN TEMPERATURE
400°
BAKING TIME
15-20 minutes
NUMBER OF SERVINGS
About 6

¼ of a minute. Spoon-drop the batter over the berries. Bake for 15 to 20 minutes, until biscuit dough is lightly browned.
Serve hot as in 1.

CHOICE BLUEBERRY COBBLER

3 cups fresh or dry-packed frozen blueberries
1 cup granulated sugar
2 teaspoons lemon juice
1 teaspoon arrowroot
¼ cup shortening
1 egg, at room temperature
1 cup all-purpose flour
1 teaspoon double-acting baking powder
¼ teaspoon salt
½ teaspoon cinnamon
⅓ cup milk, at room temperature
1 teaspoon vanilla extract
2 tablespoons hot melted butter
OVEN TEMPERATURE
400°
BAKING TIME
25-30 minutes
NUMBER OF SERVINGS
6-8

Wash and drain blueberries. Preheat oven to 400°. Combine blueberries with ½ cup sugar, lemon juice, arrowroot, and ¾ cup of water in a stainless steel or enamel saucepan. Bring to boil and stir to dissolve sugar. Simmer for 3 to 4 minutes. Pour berries into shallow, greased, 1½-quart ovenproof casserole dish. Cream shortening, gradually adding remaining ½ cup sugar until mixture is fluffy. Beat egg thoroughly, until light and lemon-colored; then blend it gently with the butter-sugar mixture.
Sift flour and measure. Resift with baking powder, salt, and cinnamon. Add dry ingredients slowly to shortening mixture, alternating with additions of the milk until all is used. Blend in the vanilla. Spread batter over top of berries, or drop by spoonfuls. Dribble melted butter over top. Bake for about 25-30 minutes.
Serve warm with whipped cream, ice cream, hot Lemon Sauce (See page 131), or Vanilla Sauce (See page 132).

NOTE: For variation, cake flour may be substituted for all-purpose flour in the pastry (increase amount by 2 tablespoonfuls), almond extract may be substituted for vanilla, or 1 teaspoon grated lemon rind may be substituted for 2 teaspoons of lemon juice. Cornstarch mixed with small amount of water may be substituted for arrowroot.

BLUEBERRY CRUNCH

INGREDIENTS
4 cups fresh or dry-packed
frozen blueberries
¾ cup all-purpose flour
½ cup granulated sugar
¼ teaspoon salt
1 teaspoon double-acting
baking powder
⅓ cup butter, at room
temperature
1 teaspoon grated lemon peel
1 teaspoon lemon juice
½ cup packed light
brown sugar
¼ teaspoon cinnamon

OVEN TEMPERATURE
375°

BAKING TIME
25-30 minutes

NUMBER OF SERVINGS
4-6

Wash, drain, and dry fresh blueberries; thaw frozen ones to separate. Preheat oven to 375°. Butter a shallow oven-proof baking dish about 1½ quarts in size. Mix flour, granulated sugar, salt, baking powder, and butter together, using a fork, until mixture forms even-sized crumbs. Put berries in baking dish, mixing and spreading evenly. Sprinkle with lemon peel and lemon juice. Crumble the topping over the fruit mixture. Sprinkle with the brown sugar and cinnamon. Bake for 25-30 minutes until crumb topping is golden brown. Serve warm with cream.

GEORGE'S QUICK SUGAR HOUSE DUMPLINGS

INGREDIENTS
1 cup biscuit mix
3 tablespoons granulated sugar
½ cup milk
2 tablespoons melted butter
or margarine
1 recipe Stewed Blueberries
(See page 115).

OVEN TEMPERATURE
450°

BAKING TIME
10-12 minutes

NUMBER OF SERVINGS
4

Preheat oven to 450°. Prepare stewed blueberries. Mix other ingredients together and drop by spoonfuls into the stewed fruit. Bake until dumplings are nicely browned.

BETTY'S BLUEBERRY DUMPLINGS

INGREDIENTS
4 cups fresh or dry-packed
frozen blueberries
1½ cups all-purpose flour
1 cup granulated sugar
1¼ teaspoons double-acting
baking powder
½ teaspoon salt
2 eggs, at room temperature
½ cup of milk, at room
temperature
COOKING TIME
12-14 minutes
NUMBER OF SERVINGS
6

Wash, drain, dry, or thaw blueberries. Sift and combine all dry ingredients. Beat eggs until light yellow, and combine with milk. Combine liquid and dry ingredients; stir until smooth. Heat blueberries and sugar in two cups water to boiling point. Drop batter by tablespoonfuls into boiling berries. Cover and cook for 12-14 minutes.

Serve with cream, real or artificial whipped cream, or light custard sauce (See page 132).

MABEL'S BLUEBERRY-APPLE CRISP

INGREDIENTS
2 cups fresh or dry-packed
frozen blueberries
6 large tart apples
2 teaspoons lemon juice
½ cup dark brown sugar
¾ cup oatmeal, quick cooking
½ cup all-purpose flour
¾ cup granulated sugar
½ teaspoon cinnamon
⅛ teaspoon soda
⅛ teaspoon double-acting
baking powder
½ cup melted butter, at room
temperature
OVEN TEMPERATURE
350°
BAKING TIME
1 hour
NUMBER OF SERVINGS
6

Preheat oven to 350°. Wash and drain blueberries as necessary. Butter a 2-quart ovenproof baking dish generously. Slice apples into eighths. Mix in lemon juice. Mix apples and blueberries in baking dish. Sprinkle fruit evenly with the brown sugar. In mixing bowl, combine oatmeal, flour, granulated sugar, cinnamon, soda, baking powder, and butter. Mix with a fork until evenly crumbled. Sprinkle crumb mixture over berries and apples in pan. Bake for one hour, or until top crust is nicely browned. Serve warm with vanilla ice cream. If you have leftovers, serve cold with Lemon Sauce (See page 131), or sharp yellow cheese.

Desserts

SUGGESTIONS FOR QUICK AND EASY
BLUEBERRY DESSERTS

(You don't need instructions on how to prepare these.)

Fresh blueberries with honey.

Stewed blueberries, with or without cream. (Just cook as many berries as you wish, in a *small* amount of water to prevent burning, until they are soft; then sweeten to taste.)

Half-melon (any kind) filled with blueberries, sugared or not.

Blueberries, sugared and crushed, and served over ice cream.

Blueberries topped with custard sauce. (You can use vanilla pudding, thinned with milk, or custard sauce, as described on page 132).

Fresh or frozen blueberries, each portion mixed thoroughly with a little lemon juice and enough blackberry liqueur to moisten them, chilled for several hours before serving.

Fresh blueberries with sour cream, mixed with confectioner's sugar and ginger to taste.

Fresh or frozen blueberries with sour cream which has been sweetened with sugar and blended with a little grated lemon peel.

Top pound cake or sponge cake with sour cream sauce and hot sugared berries, or with hot blueberry sauce (See following pages 129-130).

Top a Mary Ann (dessert shell) with honeyed blueberries and your favorite cream sauce.

Mix a cup of fresh or dry-packed frozen blueberries into batter made from package of cake mix, gingerbread mix, or coffee-cake mix, following manufacturer's directions for baking. Serve with blueberry sauce.

B- B- B- B- GOOD DESSERT
(BlueBerry Butter Bread)

INGREDIENTS
3 cups fresh blueberries
⅓ cup granulated sugar
⅛ teaspoon cinnamon
1 teaspoon lemon juice
2 slices bread
2 tablespoons soft butter
OVEN TEMPERATURE
400°
BAKING TIME
About 15 minutes
NUMBER OF SERVINGS
About 4

Preheat oven to 400°. Wash, drain, and dry blueberries between paper towels, if necessary. Pour berries into bowl and add sugar, cinnamon, lemon juice. Stir to mix. Pour into ovenproof dish about 9"x5"x2". Butter bread and cut into triangles. Place bread over the berries with the buttered side up. Bake for 15 minutes, or until berries begin to bubble and the bread is lightly toasted.
Serve with thick cream.

FRENCH BLUEBERRY PUDDING - CAKE

INGREDIENTS
2 cups fresh or dry-packed frozen blueberries
1 cup all-purpose flour
3 eggs, at room temperature
¾ cup confectioner's sugar
1¼ cups milk, boiled
⅛ teaspoon salt
1 tablespoon vanilla extract
OVEN TEMPERATURE
350°
BAKING TIME
About 1 hour
NUMBER OF SERVINGS
About 6

Preheat oven to 350°. Wash, drain, and dry blueberries between paper towels, or defrost enough to separate blueberries, if necessary. Butter a flan ring or case (or use a shallow glass pie plate).
Vigorously mix all ingredients excepting the blueberries and ¼ cup sugar. Pour half the batter in the pan. Bake for two minutes only. Remove from oven and cover with blueberries first, then the remaining batter. Smooth the top over with a spatula. Return to the oven and bake for one hour, or until the cake has puffed up and turned a golden brown. Sprinkle with remaining sugar.
Serve as soon as possible before shrinkage takes place (as with a souffle).

BLUEBERRY BROWN BETTY

INGREDIENTS
3 cups fresh, dry-packed
frozen, or drained canned
blueberries
1 egg, at room temperature
¼ teaspoon salt
½ cup milk, at room
temperature
4 slices stale bread
¾ cup granulated sugar
Juice of half a lemon
2 tablespoons confectioner's
sugar
⅛ teaspoon each of cinnamon
and nutmeg
2 tablespoons butter or
margarine (for griddle)
OVEN TEMPERATURE
350°
BAKING TIME
About 45 minutes
NUMBER OF SERVINGS
About 4

Preheat oven to 350°. Wash, drain, dry fresh berries, or defrost frozen, drain canned berries. Then, in medium mixing bowl, mix together the egg, ⅛ teaspoon salt, and the milk. Heat a heavy griddle or frying pan, buttering it generously. Dip each slice of bread in the egg-milk mixture and brown on both sides (lightly.) Cut each slice of bread into quarters and set aside.

In a stainless steel or enamel sauce pan, mix blueberries with granulated sugar, the remaining salt, and the lemon juice. Cook for 12 minutes. Pour berry mixture into square or round ovenproof baking dish about 9-10 inches in breadth. Cover berry mixture with layer of bread squares, sprinkle with confectioner's sugar and spices. Bake for approximately 45 minutes. Serve hot with Lemon Sauce or Hard Sauce (See pages 131-132).

BLUEBERRY INDIAN PUDDING

Everyone clamours to know what one can do with *dried blueberries*. Well, actually, you can use dried blueberries almost anywhere you might use raisins. *The difficulty is not how to cook them, but how to come by them!* But those who have access to wild blueberry fields and have tried drying their excess crop may be pleased with this recipe. A real New England Indian Pudding takes *days* to make and requires a gallon or more of milk, but I think you'll be satisfied with this foreshortened version of the original dish. Remember that Indian Pudding wheys, that is, it separates somewhat. Don't let this distress you in your pudding. It's supposed to do this.

INGREDIENTS
1 cup dried blueberries
1 quart of milk, cold
¼ cup yellow cornmeal
¼ cup granulated sugar
⅛ teaspoon baking soda
¾ teaspoon salt
¾ teaspoon ground ginger
½ teaspoon cinnamon
½ cup best grade, dark unsulphured molasses
2 tablespoons butter, at room temperature
1 egg, at room temperature
OVEN TEMPERATURE
250°
BAKING TIME
3 hours
NUMBER OF SERVINGS
About 6

In top of a double boiler, scald 2 cups of milk. Stir cornmeal, a little at a time, into the hot milk. Cook and stir in the top of double boiler over hot water for 15-20 minutes, or until thick. Remove from heat. Beat egg and set it aside.

Preheat your oven to 250°. Now mix together remaining dry ingredients, including blueberries, and stir into the cornmeal mixture. Add molasses, butter, and the egg, mixing well. Pour into a buttered 1-quart casserole dish. Without stirring, pour over the contents the remaining two cups of cold milk. Bake for three hours. Serve with vanilla ice cream, Hard Sauce (See page 132), or whipped cream dusted with freshly grated nutmeg.

BLUEBERRY TAPIOCA PARFAIT

INGREDIENTS
1 cup fresh or dry-packed
frozen blueberries
1 egg, at room temperature
6 tablespoons granulated sugar
2 cups milk, at room
temperature
½ teaspoon salt
¼ teaspoon nutmeg
3 tablespoons quick-cooking
tapioca
4 tablespoons confectioner's
sugar
Few drops of vanilla extract
1 teaspoon grated lemon peel
2 teaspoons lemon juice
1 cup heavy cream, cold
NUMBER OF SERVINGS
4-6

Wash, drain, and dry blueberries between paper towels. Sweeten them with confectioner's sugar. Separate egg. Whip egg white until foamy. Add to it half the granulated sugar, a little at a time, beating until egg white stands in soft peaks. Set aside. Now mix egg yolk, milk, tapioca, the rest of the granulated sugar, salt, and nutmeg in a saucepan. Place pan over medium heat and let mixture come to a boil, stirring all the time. Pour a little of the milk mixture into the egg white and blend. Add remainder of milk mixture all at once, stirring steadily. Add vanilla, lemon rind, and lemon juice, stirring to blend. Cool for 20 minutes. Whip cream until it stands in peaks. Add all but 4 spoonfuls to the pudding mixture at end of cooling period.

Fill parfait glasses with alternate layers of pudding and blueberries, beginning with berries and ending with them. Top each glass with a glob of the remaining whipped cream. Add a green leaf or two for decoration.

BLUEBERRY CHARLOTTE RUSSE

INGREDIENTS
1 pint fresh blueberries
1 teaspoon lemon juice
12 ladyfingers
1 envelope unflavored gelatine
1 cup milk, cold
½ pint heavy whipping
cream, cold
½ cup granulated sugar
⅛ teaspoon salt
2 tablespoons vanilla extract
2 egg whites
NUMBER OF SERVINGS
4-6

Wash and drain blueberries, if necessary. Then crush and strain them, or purée in electric blender with lemon juice. Line a mold with split lady-fingers. Soften gelatine in half a cup of cold milk. When completely softened (about three minutes), add rest of milk and heat slowly just to boiling point, stirring constantly. Remove from heat. Add blueberries, sugar, salt, and vanilla, stirring until sugar is dissolved. Cool in pan, then chill until just beginning to set.

Beat egg whites with dash of salt until stiff. Separately, whip the cream. Fold egg whites and whipped cream into gelatine mix. Pour mixture into mold, being careful not to disturb ladyfingers. Chill until set (several hours).

When ready to serve, invert mold on a serving plate. Serve with a topping of whipped cream and Thick Blueberry Topping (See page 136).

BLUEBERRY BAVARIAN CREAM

INGREDIENTS
1 package frozen blueberries
(about 10 ounces)
1 tablespoon unflavored
gelatine
½ cup lemon juice
2⅓ cups granulated sugar
¼ teaspoon salt
1 egg white
¾ cup heavy cream, cold
NUMBER OF SERVINGS
6

Thaw, drain, and crush blueberries. Soften gelatine in ¼ cup cold water. Dissolve in half a cup of boiling water. Add lemon juice and ⅓ cup of sugar. Cool. Add drained blueberries. Chill until thick, but not set. Add salt to egg white and beat until soft peaks form. Add two tablespoons sugar, beating constantly until stiff. Whip cream until it stands in peaks. Fold whipped cream and beaten egg white into gelatine mixture.
Pour into 1½-quart mold, or six individual molds. Chill until set.

BLUEBERRY RICE CRÈME

INGREDIENTS
1 cup Blueberry Sauce
(See. page 129)
⅔ cup quick-cooked rice
⅓ cup granulated sugar
1⅓ cups milk
½ teaspoon salt
1 teaspoon vanilla extract
⅓ cup slivered, blanched almonds
½ cup whipping cream, cold
COOKING TIME
7-9 minutes
CHILLING TIME
One hour
NUMBER OF SERVINGS
4-6

Boil rice, milk, sugar, salt in uncovered saucepan for 7-9 minutes, stirring and fluffing as needed, until rice is light and fluffy. Remove from heat, cover, and let stand for 10 minutes. Add vanilla. Fold in nuts. Pour into bowl and chill for an hour. Whip cream and fold into rice mixture.

Serve with Blueberry Sauce (See page 129).

PATRIOT'S CAKE

Here's a special way to use blueberries for entertaining on a special occasion such as the Fourth of July, Washington's Birthday, or Veteran's Day.

INGREDIENTS
FOR THE CAKE
1 cup blueberries, fresh or dry-packed frozen
3 cups cake flour
4 teaspoons double-acting baking powder
½ teaspoon salt
6 egg whites, at room temperature.
1¾ cups granulated sugar
1 cup butter or margarine, at room temperature
1 cup milk, at room temperature
1 teaspoon vanilla

Wash and drain blueberries, if necessary, patting dry with paper towels. Toss in small amount of flour to cover. Preheat oven to 350°. Grease a pan 15"x10"x2" (Approx.); lightly flour the bottom and line with paper. Measure sifted flour. Resift twice more with baking powder and salt. Whip egg whites until stiff, but not dry. Sift sugar. Cream butter well. Gradually add sifted sugar to butter and continue creaming until light and fluffy. Add flour mixture to butter mixture a small amount at a time, alternating with portions of milk until all is used. Stir the batter until smooth after each

OVEN TEMPERATURE
350°
BAKING TIME
30 minutes
NUMBER OF SERVINGS
About 3 dozen

INGREDIENTS FOR
ICING AND
DECORATIONS
1 cup vegetable shortening,
at room temperature
¼ teaspoon salt
3 cups confectioner's sugar
4 tablespoons cream
1 tablespoon vanilla extract
1 cup large blueberries
(Approx.), preferably frozen
by dry-pack method
1 cup firm red strawberries
(Approx.)
1 cup miniature white
marshmallows (Approx.)

addition. Beat in the vanilla extract. Gently fold egg whites into the cake batter, then the blueberries. Spread batter into large greased pan.

Bake for 30 or 35 minutes until done. Cool cake for about 10 minutes, then remove carefully from pan to tray upon which it is to be served. This is most easily done by inverting over the tray. Ice while still warm.

Make a paper pattern the size of your cake. Draw off a square to represent the blue field of the flag, and stripes to represent the American flag's original 13 stripes.

Cream the vegetable shortening with the salt. Add the sugar, beating until smooth and fluffy. Beat in the cream. Add vanilla. (This frosting does not have to be cooked. If too thick, add milk or cream, if too thin, add more confectioner's sugar.) Spread icing evenly over entire cake, keeping it smooth by dipping your spatula frequently into hot water.

Using the paper pattern as a guide, place 13 white candles in small white party holders in a circle in the section which is to represent your field of blue. Place large blueberries over the field and around the candles until the field is covered. For red stripes of the flag, cover with red strawberries. Leave white stripes with frosting representing the white of the flag, or decorate with white miniature marshmallows.

Place in refrigerator if the cake cannot be served at once. Light candles just before cake is brought to the table.

GRACE'S BLUEBERRY CAKE

INGREDIENTS

2 cups fresh, dry-packed frozen, or drained canned blueberries

½ cup granulated sugar

¼ cup shortening, at room temperature

1 egg, at room temperature

1½ cups all-purpose flour

2½ teaspoons double-acting baking powder

¼ teaspoon salt

½ cup milk, at room temperature

½ teaspoon lemon extract

OVEN TEMPERATURE
375°

BAKING TIME
30 minutes

NUMBER OF SERVINGS
8-10

Grease and flour a spring-form cake pan. Prepare blueberries, washing, draining, defrosting, as necessary, and patting dry. Toss berries in small amount of flour to cover. Crush about ⅓ of them. Refrigerate until ready to use. Preheat oven to 375°.

Cream shortening and sugar until granular appearance disappears. Beat egg vigorously and add to the shortening mix. Sift flour and measure. Resift with baking powder and salt. Add dry ingredients to shortening mix a little at a time, alternating with additions of milk until all is used. Add lemon extract and stir to mix. Fold blueberries into the batter. Pour into cake form.

Bake for 30 minutes, or until top springs back when touched with finger, or until cake tester inserted comes out clean. Remove to cake rack to cool before removing to serving plate.

Garnish with a light topping of confectioner's sugar, or cover with Maple or Butter Frosting (See page 134).

BEA'S BLUEBERRY GINGERBREAD TREAT

INGREDIENTS

¾ cup fresh or dry-packed
frozen blueberries
2 cups all-purpose flour
1 teaspoon baking soda
1½ teaspoons ginger
½ teaspoon salt
⅓ cup butter or margarine,
at room temperature
1 egg, at room temperature
½ cup brown sugar
1 cup molasses, warm
½ cupful sour cream

OVEN TEMPERATURE
350°

BAKING TIME
40 minutes

NUMBER OF SERVINGS
6-9

Preheat oven to 350°. Butter a 9-inch square cake pan. Wash, drain, and dry fresh blueberries, or defrost frozen ones just enough to separate. Toss in small amount of flour, then set aside. Sift and measure flour. Resift with baking soda, ginger, and salt. Cream butter until soft. Add sugar slowly, beating thoroughly as you add. Beat egg until light and lemon-colored. Add to butter-sugar combination, mixing well. Combine molasses and sour cream, mixing well. Add to butter mixture. Add liquid ingredients to dry ingredients, stirring just enough to make a smooth batter. With a light touch, fold in the blueberries.
Spoon batter into pan. Bake for 40 minutes, or until cake pulls away from sides of pan.
Serve warm, with butter.

Coville

DOROTHY'S BLUEBERRY TRIFLE

INGREDIENTS
⅓ cup whole fresh blueberries
1 layer of sponge cake,
fresh or stale
½ cup sherry, rum, or brandy
½ cup toasted, slivered almonds
½ cup blueberry jam
(See page 137)
Custard Sauce
(See page 132)
1 cup heavy cream, cold
NUMBER OF SERVINGS
About 6

Make Custard Sauce according to directions on page 132. Place cake in bottom of serving dish. Saturate the cake with liqueur. Refrigerate until ready to use. Then spread the top with blueberry jam. Stud it with almonds. Pour custard over the top. Whip cream (sweeten, if you wish) and pile on top. Decorate with green leaves and fresh blueberries.

BLUEBERRY FLUMMERY

INGREDIENTS
1 quart fresh or dry-packed
frozen blueberries
⅔ cup granulated sugar
⅛ teaspoon salt
1 tablespoon cornstarch
2 tablespoons lemon juice
2 cups cubed plain cake
(sponge or chiffon)
1 cup commercial
sour cream, cold
NUMBER OF SERVINGS
4-6

Wash, drain, and dry blueberries between paper towels, if necessary. Place berries, sugar, and salt in saucepan containing 1 cup water, and bring to a boil. Reduce heat to simmer. Mix cornstarch in 3 tablespoons of water; add to blueberry-sugar mixture, and cook, stirring until thickened and clear (about 12 minutes.) Stir in lemon juice and cool, then refrigerate. Line bottoms of 4-6 dessert dishes with cake cubes. Cover with blueberry mix. Top with sour cream to serve.

AUNT EM'S BLUEBERRY TORTE

INGREDIENTS
3 cups fresh or dry-packed
frozen blueberries
1¾ cups dry, ready-to-eat
cereal (Shredded Wheat, Wheat
Bits, Wheat Chex, or similar
crunchy, unsweetened type)
1¼ cups all-purpose flour
1 teaspoon salt
¾ cup butter or margarine
Juice of 1 orange
1 teaspoon grated orange peel
1 pint whipping cream, cold
3 teaspoons
confectioner's sugar
½ teaspoon vanilla extract
OVEN TEMPERATURE
350°
BAKING TIME
12 minutes (about)
NUMBER OF SERVINGS
8

Preheat oven to 350°. Crush cereal into crumbs with rolling pin and measure. Sift flour and measure. Resift with salt. Cut butter into flour mixture with a pastry blender to the coarseness of grain. Add cereal and mix. Stir in orange juice and orange peel. With floured hands, lift from bowl patting into ball shape, and place on floured board, turning several times and pressing into elongated oval. Divide into three equal-sized portions, rolling each into a ball. Refrigerate while you prepare next step.

Wash, drain, and pat dry the blueberries with paper towels, if necessary. Toss berries in small amount of confectioner's sugar. Whip cream until stiff. Stir in vanilla and sugar. Fold blueberries lightly into whipped cream. Store in refrigerator until ready to use. Remove dough balls from refrigerator. On floured board, roll each into a 9-inch circle and place on large, ungreased baking sheet. Prick each circle with fork to avoid bubbles in baking. Bake for 12 minutes, or until brown. Cool on cake rack.

Remove one round to serving plate. Cover it generously with half the whipped cream-blueberry mixture. Add the second layer. Cover with remaining filling. Put on the final layer. Chill until ready to serve.

At serving time, top with Orange or Brandy Sauce (See pages 130-133).

BLUEBERRY SHORTCAKE

There are as many ways to make blueberry shortcake as there are for strawberry shortcake, and each style has its proponents. Those who sponsor a sweet cake base look with scorn upon those who champion biscuit dough, and even the biscuit supporters are divided into two camps — those who like a sweetened dough, and those who want it salty and buttery. Looked at askance by both these groups are the exponents of a crisp, salty pie dough.

The filling and the topping come in for almost as much criticism and appraisal. Shall the shortcake be served with whipped cream, plain cream, or some other blown-up topping? Shall the berries be served whole or crushed, sweetened with confectioner's sugar, granulated sugar, brown sugar, maple syrup, liqueur, or nothing? And what is the proper number of berries to serve? Does all of the garnishing belong on top or between layers? And so on.

If you want to get down to basic facts, I suppose the biscuit backers represent the true gourmets. A shortcake by any dictionary's definition comes out a biscuit heavy with shortening and often sweetened, and usually topped or filled with fruit. The cake eaters are close to the center, too, when they aver that a cake is a cake and shouldn't be confused with bread or pie.

I might as well tell you right now, however, that I'm a *pie dough* advocate. And though I've suggested artificial whipped toppings in many of the recipes in this book as an alternative to whipped cream (because there are some really quite nice ones on the market today), in the realm of the shortcake, I'm adamant. *Nothing but really rich whipped cream is adequate!* And berries can be whole, or partially crushed, but *they must be fresh!*

I'll concede that I've tasted some delicious shortcake made with biscuit-type dough, and for this reason I've included one of my favorites in this book. With some reluctance, I've included one cake dough recipe, too, for who am I to impose my taste upon another with no choice if he doesn't concur?

But if you use cake dough, *please* make your cake "from scratch", won't you? Don't serve your family and friends any of those soggy little dishes made from "store-bought" cake rounds, marshmallow garnish, and a little lost berry or two tucked in somewhere. (How many times I've fallen for the restaurant's description of its pièce-de-résistance — strawberry shortcake, only to be served something of this sort, or a limp piece of layer cake, with artificial filling, and a single, huge, long-forgotten berry on top, served up from the depths of a freezer.)

Never scrimp on a shortcake — give the dish all the consideration and investment of time and money that it deserves!

MY MOTHER'S BLUEBERRY SHORTCAKE

INGREDIENTS
2 cups fresh blueberries,
preferably wild
2 cups all-purpose flour
1 rounded teaspoon salt
⅔ cup shortening
5 to 7 tablespoons ice water
1 teaspoon lemon juice
2 cups heavy whipping
cream, cold
1 teaspoon vanilla
½ cup confectioner's sugar
3-6 tablespoons
granulated sugar
OVEN TEMPERATURE
425°
BAKING TIME
12-15 minutes
NUMBER OF SERVINGS
4-6

Preheat oven to 425°. Sift the flour before measuring. Then resift flour with the salt. Cut in shortening with pastry blender until pieces are size of small peas. Sprinkle water, a tablespoonful at a time, over the mixture, each time lightly tossing the part of the mix reached, with a fork. Move about the bowl, sprinkling a different section each time until all has been moistened. Form a ball of dough, handling lightly. Put dough in refrigerator to chill for at least two hours, if possible. Take out about an hour before rolling. When ready to roll, *lightly* flour a pastry cloth and your rolling pin. (Use a glass pin filled with chipped ice and covered with a roller "stocking" for the very best results.) Flatten ball of dough slightly and roll ⅛ inch thick. Now, with a pastry wheel, cut dough into 2" x 4" strips. Prick each piece about 2 to 3 times with fork.

Place these strips on a cookie sheet and bake for 12 to 15 minutes, until lightly browned. Set the pastry strips aside until ready to use. If this period is to be very long, a pie safe, bread box, or cake box is recommended.

Prepare berries about an hour before serving. Wash, drain, and pat them dry between paper towels. Toss them in a little granulated sugar to cover and sprinkle them with lemon juice. Leave about half the berries whole, but crush the other half so there will be some juice. Refrigerate until time to use.

Now you're ready to whip your cream. Before you do so, see that all the utensils to be used are ice cold — bowls, beaters, spoons, etc. For best results, these utensils should be left in the refrigerator for several hours, but you can speed things up by putting them in the freezer compartment for a few minutes, then wiping them dry before using.

If possible, use an electric mixer to whip cream, whipping just until it forms large soft peaks. (Too much whipping and you'll have butter.) Start at medium speed, and when the cream begins to thicken, change to low speed. Do not overbeat. Stop mixer when cream is of right consistency and add vanilla and confectioner's sugar, stirring just enough to blend. Amount of sugar will depend upon your own taste. Sample the whipped cream as you add to be sure, remembering that your blueberries, even though sugared, will be a little tart, and your pie crust a little salty.

When ready to serve, place several pie crust strips on saucers or salad plates (Mother used a *soup* plate!), breaking another strip into pieces on top. Top the crust strips with a generous portion of whipped cream, then with some crushed berries, and a generous portion of whole berries.
NOTE: You will find this dough crisp and flaky. The unusual amount of salt "takes away" from the oversweet taste of whipped cream and sugared berries, so common to many berry shortcakes.

CAKE-LOVER'S BLUEBERRY SHORTCAKE

INGREDIENTS
2 cups fresh blueberries
1½ cups cake flour
2 teaspoons double-acting
baking powder
¼ teaspoon salt
⅓ cup butter
¾ cup granulated sugar
1 teaspoon vanilla
3 eggs, at room temperature
½ cup milk, at
room temperature
1 cup whipping cream, cold
¼ cup confectioner's sugar
(about)
OVEN TEMPERATURE
375°
BAKING TIME
20 minutes
NUMBER OF SERVINGS
6

Wash, drain, and pat blueberries dry between paper towels. Toss in enough confectioner's sugar to cover. Grease and flour two 8-inch cake pans. Preheat oven to 375°.

Sift cake flour and measure. Resift cake flour with baking powder and salt. In another bowl, cream butter until soft. Add vanilla. Now cream butter mixture and granulated sugar thoroughly, whipping until light. Separate eggs. Add, one at a time, the 3 egg yolks, beating thoroughly until light and fluffy. Add the dry ingredients by thirds to the egg-and-shortening mixture, alternating with equivalent amounts of milk. Beat just enough to blend.

Spread evenly in pans. Bake for 20 minutes, or until top of cake springs back to the touch, or until a cake tester inserted comes out dry and clean. Remove to cake rack to cool before removing to serving plate. Dust with confectioner's sugar.

Prepare whipped cream as directed in previous recipe.

When ready to serve, spread half of the whipped cream and berries on top of one layer of cake, top with second layer, and cover surface with remaining whipped cream and the berries.

NOTE: This cake is best served at once. Even if you refrigerate it before serving, you cannot avoid a certain sogginess if service is delayed.

POPULAR BLUEBERRY SHORTCAKE

INGREDIENTS

4 cups fresh blueberries
2 cups all-purpose flour
¼ cup granulated sugar
¼ cup confectioner's sugar
(about)
2 teaspoons double-acting
baking powder
½ teaspoon salt
1 large egg, at
room temperature
½ cup light cream, at
room temperature
¼ pound butter or margarine,
at room temperature
1 cup heavy cream, cold
1 teaspoon vanilla extract

OVEN TEMPERATURE
450°

BAKING TIME
About 10 minutes

NUMBER OF SERVINGS
6

Preheat oven to 450°. Wash, drain, and pat berries dry with paper towels. Toss them in half the granulated sugar listed. Crush about one-third of them. Refrigerate until ready to use. Sift flour. Resift with remaining granulated sugar, baking powder, and salt. Cut in butter until it resembles texture of corn meal. Beat egg and combine with light cream, stirring to mix. Add liquid ingredients to dry ingredients, mixing with a fork, just until the dough clings together. Remove dough to lightly floured pastry board. Roll to about ¾-inch thickness. With a large floured biscuit cutter, cut out as many biscuits as you can (About 6). Place biscuits (or shortcakes) on an ungreased cookie sheet. Brush tops with a little milk or cream. Bake for about 10 minutes or until golden brown.
While shortcakes are baking, whip your cream and flavor with vanilla and confectioner's sugar (See page 98).

When shortcakes are ready, split them, spread with soft butter, spoon berries over bottom layers, replace tops, garnish generously with whipped cream and more berries. Serve warm.

OLD-FASHIONED BLUEBERRY SHORTCAKE

INGREDIENTS
3 cups fresh blueberries
3 cups all-purpose flour
3 teaspoons double-acting
baking powder
½ teaspoon salt
¼ pound of butter or margarine
1 egg, at room temperature
⅔ cup milk (about), at
room temperature
½ cup granulated sugar
¼ cup confectioner's sugar
1 pint heavy cream, cold
OVEN TEMPERATURE
400°-450°, depending upon
method used
BAKING TIME
20-30 minutes, depending
upon method used
NUMBER OF SERVINGS
6

Preheat oven to 400°. Wash, drain, and pat berries dry between paper towels. Mix berries with the granulated sugar and refrigerate until ready to use.

Sift flour and measure. Resift with baking powder and salt. Cut in butter with a pastry blender until mixture becomes texture of cornmeal. Beat egg until light and lemon-colored. Add egg to dry ingredients along with enough of the milk to make a soft dough. Do this, mixing very lightly with a fork; you do not want to overhandle. At this point you may wish to prepare shortcake in one of two ways:

1. Divide dough in half. On a lightly floured board, roll one portion to fit the bottom of an ungreased 9-inch cake pan. Cover this round with the sugared blueberries. Roll remaining dough to same size as first, and put on top of berries. Bake at 400° for 30 minutes, or until dough is lightly browned. Serve warm with confectioner's sugar and heavy cream (unwhipped).

2. On lightly floured pastry board, roll all the dough in a circle to fit an ungreased 9-inch cake pan. Bake this loaf at 450° for about 20 minutes, or until dough is lightly browned. Remove from oven and cool for five minutes. Then, with a serrated knife, while still warm, split into two layers, lifting the top off carefully. Butter the halves as you would a biscuit. Cover the lower half with sugared blueberries. Place upper half on top of the blueberries and sprinkle generously with confectioner's sugar.

Serve warm with heavy cream (unwhipped).

"MOD" BLUEBERRY SHORTCAKE

INGREDIENTS

2 cups fresh blueberries
½ cup orange liqueur (Triple Sec, Cointreau)
1 teaspoon grated lemon peel
1 cup granulated sugar
5 eggs, at room temperature
1 tablespoon lemon juice
1 cup cake flour
1½ teaspoons double-acting baking powder
¼ teaspoon salt
1 cup whipping cream, cold
¼ cup confectioner's sugar (about)

OVEN TEMPERATURE
325°

BAKING TIME
1 hour

NUMBER OF SERVINGS
8-10

Preheat oven to 325°. Wash, drain, and dry berries between paper towels. Toss in small amount of granulated sugar. Pour over them 2 tablespoonsful of orange liqueur. Refrigerate until ready to use.

Grate lemon peel. Sift sugar; mix with lemon rind. Separate eggs. Beat egg yolks until light and lemon-colored. Gradually beat in granulated sugar, then a quarter cup of boiling water. Cool, then beat in the lemon juice. Sift and measure the cake flour. Resift with the baking powder and salt. Gradually add the dry ingredients to the liquid ingredients; stir batter just enough to blend. Beat egg whites until they stand up in soft peaks but are not dry. Fold egg whites lightly into the batter.

Pour batter into cake pan. With spatula, draw a line through the batter to destroy any bubbles. Bake for about one hour. Cake is ready when breaks in crust are dry.

Invert the cake over a bottle or funnel, and let remain in this position for about one hour (or more) before removing from pan (just as you do angel cake). With a sharp knife, make 5 or 6 small cuts in the cake and pour in all but one teaspoonful of the remaining orange liqueur.

To serve, fill center with blueberries and top with whipped cream, prepared with confectioner's sugar, as on page 98, using one teaspoonful of orange liqueur instead of vanilla as flavoring.

SALLY'S BLUEBERRY TORTE

INGREDIENTS
1½ cups blueberry jam
(See page 137)
1½ cups cake flour
1½ cups granulated sugar
2 teaspoons double-acting
baking powder
½ teaspoon salt
½ cup shortening, at
room temperature
4 eggs, at room temperature
½ cup milk, at
room temperature
1 teaspoon vanilla
¼ cup blanched,
slivered almonds
OVEN TEMPERATURE
350°
BAKING TIME
About 35 minutes
NUMBER OF SERVINGS
About 8

Preheat oven to 350°. Sift cake flour and measure. Resift with salt and baking powder. Cream shortening and ⅔ cup sugar together until smooth and fluffy. Separate eggs. Set whites aside. Beat yolks until light and lemon-colored. Add egg yolks to shortening mix. Beat thoroughly. Add dry ingredients to the shortening mixture, alternating with additions of milk, beating well between additions. Stir in vanilla.

Pour batter into two 9-inch, ungreased, spring-form cake pans. (If you must use regular cake pans, line bottoms with waxed paper.) Bake for about 20 minutes. Meanwhile, beat egg whites until fluffy. Continue to beat egg whites, adding the remaining ¾ cup of sugar a little at a time until egg whites form stiff peaks.

Open oven door and spread meringue over the two layers of cake. Sprinkle almonds over tops of meringues. Continue to bake for about 15 minutes longer, until meringue is light brown. Cool layers on cake rack. When cool, remove sides of pans. Put one layer on serving dish. Spread blueberry jam over the top. Top with second layer of cake. Dust top of torte with confectioner's sugar. Decorate with a few green leaves and a cluster of whole blueberries. Frost sides with whipped cream, if you wish.

BLUEBERRY CHEESECAKE

INGREDIENTS
FOR CRUST
1½ cups graham cracker
crumbs
⅓ cup ground almonds
⅓ cup granulated sugar
½ cup melted butter
3 tablespoons cream
NUMBER OF SERVINGS
8

Mix all ingredients thoroughly. Line an 8-inch cake pan (*not* a spring pan) with the dough, patting firmly to cover bottom and sides. Chill in refrigerator until firm.

INGREDIENTS
FOR FILLING
2 envelopes unflavored gelatine
3 eggs, at room temperature
1 cup granulated sugar
½ cup milk, at
room temperature
1 teaspoon vanilla
Dash of salt
2 cups creamed cottage cheese
1 cup heavy whipping
cream, cold
COOKING TIME
About 5 minutes

Soften gelatine in water. Dissolve in top of double boiler over hot water. Separate eggs. Beat egg yolks and combine with sugar and milk. Add to gelatine mixture in double boiler. Cook slowly, stirring constantly, until mixture thickens slightly (about 5 minutes). Remove from heat, add the vanilla and salt and cool. Beat mixture with electric beater until it is smooth. Sieve cottage cheese into large bowl. Pour cooled gelatine mixture into the cheese dish, stirring thoroughly to mix. Chill, stirring occasionally. Beat egg whites until stiff, but not dry. Whip cream until stiff. Fold egg whites and then the whipped cream into the gelatine mixture. Pour filling into the crumb crust. Chill until firm.

INGREDIENTS
FOR TOPPING
1-1½ cups fresh or frozen
blueberries (optional)
1 cup Blueberry Glaze
(See page 127).
2 tablespoons melted butter
1 tablespoon light brown sugar
½ cup graham cracker crumbs
¼ teaspoon nutmeg

Mix last four ingredients thoroughly, sprinkling over top of cake, and chill. When ready to serve, top with whole blueberries and Blueberry Glaze (Page 127).

BLUEBERRY UPSIDE DOWN CAKE

INGREDIENTS
1½ cups fresh or dry-packed
frozen blueberries
¾ cup light brown sugar
⅓ cup butter or margarine,
at room temperature
½ cup granulated sugar
1 egg, at room temperature
1½ cups sifted cake flour
¼ teaspoon salt
2 teaspoons double-acting
baking powder
⅓ cup orange juice (or milk)
1 teaspoon grated orange peel
(if orange juice is used)
OVEN TEMPERATURE
400°
BAKING TIME
30 minutes
NUMBER OF SERVINGS
6

Preheat oven to 400°. Wash, drain, and pat blueberries dry with paper towels, or defrost just enough to separate. Grease a 9-inch round or square cake pan. Simmer brown sugar and 1 tablespoon butter in small saucepan for five minutes. Pour into greased pan, and spread over bottom. Add blueberries, spreading evenly over mixture. Cream remaining butter and granulated sugar until light and fluffy. Beat egg, then add it to creamed sugar and butter mix. Add orange peel to mix, and beat thoroughly. Sift and mix all dry ingredients and add to mixture in small portions, alternating with orange juice. Gently spoon mixture over berries in pan, spreading evenly.

Bake for approximately 30 minutes until top springs back when touched. Loosen sides with knife or spatula and turn out on a serving dish, fruit side up. Serve warm with whipped cream, Vanilla Sauce, and/or Blueberry Sauce (See pages 129-132).

GRANNY WEAVER'S HEAVENLY JAM CAKE

INGREDIENTS
¾ cup blueberry jam
(See page 137)
3 cups all-purpose flour
2 tablespoons double-acting
baking powder
½ cup cornstarch
1 teaspoon salt
½ pound butter
2 cups granulated sugar
12 egg whites
1 cup milk, at room
temperature
2 teaspoons lemon juice
¼ cup confectioner's
sugar (optional)
OVEN TEMPERATURE
350°
BAKING TIME
About 30 minutes
NUMBER OF SERVINGS
About 8

Preheat oven to 350°. Grease and lightly flour three 8-inch cake pans. (Line bottoms of cake tins with rounds of brown paper, if you prefer.) Sift and measure flour. Sift again with all other dry ingredients, excepting sugar. Cream butter until light and fluffy, adding sugar a little at a time until smooth and light. Add dry ingredients to butter mixture, slowly alternating with additions of milk. Add lemon juice to batter. Beat egg whites until they stand in peaks. (You'll need a *large* bowl for this.) Lightly fold in egg whites, mixing throughout. Divide batter between the three cake pans. Bake for 30 minutes, or until cake tester comes out clean and dry. Turn on cake rack to cool. Remove to serving plate. Generously spread blueberry jam between layers. Sprinkle top of cake with confectioner's sugar, or frost with Butter Frosting (See page 135).

BLUEBERRY SPICE CAKE

INGREDIENTS
1 pint fresh or dry-packed
frozen blueberries
2 cups all-purpose flour
½ teaspoon salt
2 teaspoons double-acting
baking powder
1 teaspoon baking soda
½ teaspoon each of cinnamon,
powdered cloves, allspice

Preheat oven to 375°. Wash, drain, and dry blueberries between paper towels, or defrost enough to separate berries. Toss berries in a little flour to cover. Butter and flour a 9"x13"x2" pan. Sift flour and measure. Resift with baking powder, baking soda, the spices, and salt. Cream butter and sugar. Beat egg until thick and lemon-colored and add to butter mixture. Beat well.

1 cup granulated sugar
⅓ cup soft butter or margarine
1 egg, at room temperature
3 tablespoons molasses
1 cup sour milk, at room
temperature
⅓ cup confectioner's sugar

OVEN TEMPERATURE
375°

BAKING TIME
About 30 minutes

NUMBER OF SERVINGS
About 8

Gradually beat in the molasses. Alternately add the butter-egg-molasses mixture and the sour milk to the dry ingredients, a little at a time, beating well after each addition. Fold in the blueberries.

Pour into the greased baking pan and bake for about 30 minutes. Remove from the oven when cake skewer inserted comes out clean. Cool cake in the pan on a rack, then dust with confectioner's sugar. Cut in squares to serve.

BLUEBERRY SCONES

INGREDIENTS
1 cup fresh or dry-packed
frozen blueberries
2 cups all-purpose flour
½ teaspoon salt
1 tablespoon double-acting
baking powder
2 tablespoons granulated sugar
3 tablespoons melted butter
¾ cup heavy cream

OVEN TEMPERATURE
450°

BAKING TIME
12-15 minutes

NUMBER OF SERVINGS
About 1 dozen

Preheat oven to 450°. Wash, drain, and dry blueberries between paper towels, or thaw frozen berries enough to separate. Toss lightly in a little flour to cover. Butter a large cookie sheet.

Sift flour and measure. Resift with salt, baking powder, and *one* tablespoon of sugar. Add cream and stir until dough holds together. Fold blueberries into batter.

Stir well, then with floured hands, remove dough to a floured board and roll lightly into a soft ball. Gently pat dough to ½-inch thickness. Cut into 1½-inch squares with a knife or pastry-cutter. Lift squares from board and arrange on baking sheet, separating as far as possible. Brush top of each square with butter. Use remaining tablespoonful of sugar to sprinkle over top. Bake for 12-15 minutes until golden brown. Serve hot with butter, and with Blueberry Jam (See page 137).

BLUEBERRY TEA CAKES

INGREDIENTS
1 cup fresh or dry-packed
frozen blueberries
2 cups cake flour
2 teaspoons double-acting
baking powder
Dash of salt
⅓ cup soft butter or margarine
1 cup granulated sugar
2 eggs, at room temperature
⅔ cup milk, at room
temperature
1 teaspoon vanilla
(or lemon juice)
OVEN TEMPERATURE
375°
BAKING TIME
20-25 minutes
NUMBER OF SERVINGS
1½ dozen small cupcakes,
or 9 squares

Preheat oven to 375°. Wash, drain, and dry blueberries between paper towels, then flour them lightly. Grease a 9-inch square pan or small-cup muffin pan. Sift cake flour once. Mix with baking powder and salt, sifting twice again. Cream butter thoroughly until soft and smooth. Gradually add sugar to butter, creaming until soft and fluffy. Thoroughly beat in eggs and flavoring. Add flour in small amounts at a time, alternating with small amounts of milk, until all is used, beating smooth after each addition. Fold blueberries lightly into the mix.

Pour into greased pan or muffin tins, filling two-thirds full. (If one or more muffin cups are not used, fill with water to prevent burning.) Bake 20-25 minutes or until cake tester inserted comes out clean. Frost, if desired, with a plain Butter or Maple Frosting. (See index for recipes which follow.) If pan was used, cut into 9 squares.

HELEN'S BLUEBERRY DROP COOKIES

¾ cup fresh, frozen, or
canned blueberries
1¾ cups all-purpose flour
2 teaspoons double-acting
baking powder
½ teaspoon salt
½ cup soft butter or
margarine
1 cup granulated sugar (If
syrup-packed frozen berries
are used, cut sugar to ½ cup)
2 egg yolks
1 teaspoon lemon rind
½ teaspoon lemon juice
½ cup milk or light cream
OVEN TEMPERATURE
375°
BAKING TIME
About 12 minutes
AMOUNT PRODUCED
About 2 dozen

Prepare blueberries as necessary, washing, draining, drying fresh berries, defrosting and separating frozen berries, or draining canned berries. Toss in small amount of sugar to cover (except if syrup-packed berries are used). Grease a large cookie sheet. Preheat oven to 375°.

Sift flour and measure. Resift with baking powder and salt. In another bowl, cream butter until soft. Gradually beat in sugar, and cream until granular appearance disappears. Separate eggs. Put whites away. Beat egg yolks until light and lemon-colored. Add yolks to butter mixture, beating vigorously. Stir in lemon rind. Add dry ingredients, a third at a time, to butter-sugar-berry combination, alternating with thirds of the milk, finishing with the dry ingredients. Mix to blend. Fold in blueberries.

Drop from teaspoon onto cookie sheet, about two inches apart. Bake for about 12 minutes, or until cookies are brown around the edges and golden on top. Remove from cookie sheet at once to cool on rack.

BERYL'S FAVORITE BLUEBERRY ROLL

INGREDIENTS

1 large can blueberries

1¾ cups all-purpose flour

*2½ teaspoons double-acting
baking powder*

¼ teaspoon salt

¼ cup slivered almonds

*3 tablespoons softened
shortening*

*1 tablespoon butter or
margarine*

½ teaspoon cinnamon

*½ cup milk, at room
temperature*

2 teaspoons lemon juice

OVEN TEMPERATURE

400°

BAKING TIME

About 30 minutes

NUMBER OF SERVINGS

6

Preheat oven to 400°. Drain blueberries, reserving juice. Grease an oblong glass baking pan. Sift flour and measure. Resift with baking powder and salt. Cut in shortening until mix is as fine as cornmeal. Add milk, mixing quickly to a soft but not sticky dough. Turn onto a floured board or pastry cloth and knead lightly, about 10 times, forming a smooth ball. Press to shape of pan and about ¼ inch thick. Spread blueberries evenly over dough. Sprinkle lightly with the lemon juice. Roll like a jelly roll, pressing edges together. Cut into six equal portions and space evenly in the pan. Brush top of each roll lightly with melted butter, and sprinkle lightly with cinnamon. Mix remaining lemon juice with blueberry juice and pour around the rolls. Garnish with buttered, blanched, slivered, almonds. Bake for 30 minutes or until lightly browned. Serve in individual dishes, spooning some blueberry syrup from the pan over each roll. Finish with a dollop of real or artificial whipped cream.

QUICK AND EASY BLUEBERRY ROLL

INGREDIENTS

1½ pints blueberries, fresh,
dry-packed frozen, or canned
2 packages frozen biscuits
(10 biscuits to the pack)
½ cup granulated sugar
1½ tablespoons lemon juice
Dash of cinnamon
3 tablespoons melted butter
or margarine

OVEN TEMPERATURE
400°

BAKING TIME
About 25 minutes

NUMBER OF SERVINGS
10-12

Preheat oven temperature to 400°. Wash, drain and pat dry fresh blueberries or thaw frozen ones. If canned berries are used, drain, and set juice aside. Grease a cookie sheet. Open packages and place the 20 biscuits on a lightly floured board, five to a row, edges touching. Roll into a single oblong piece about ⅓ inch thick, turning once to flour both sides. Spread blueberries over the dough. Sprinkle with the sugar, lemon juice, and cinnamon. Roll as for a jelly roll, and place, seam side down, on cookie sheet. Brush with butter.

Bake for 25 minutes or until golden brown.

Slice and serve with one of the dessert sauces described on pages 129-133, or, if canned berries were used and you have juice left over, with Blueberry Sauce (page 129).

BLUEBERRY RICE PUDDING

INGREDIENTS
½ cup fresh, frozen and thawed, or canned blueberries
½ cup rice
1 quart milk
⅓ cup softened butter or margarine
3 eggs, at room temperature
½ cup granulated sugar
1 teaspoon vanilla
¼ teaspoon salt
Dash of cinnamon

OVEN TEMPERATURE
325°

COOKING TIME
Half-hour

NUMBER OF SERVINGS
6

Prepare blueberries. Fresh or dry-packed frozen berries should be washed and dried, and tossed in small amount of sugar. Syrup-packed or canned ones should be drained. (Juice from canned berries may be used to prepare one of the blueberry drinks described elsewhere.) With butter or margarine, grease well a 1½ quart, ovenproof casserole dish.

Mix rice with 2 cups of milk in the top of a double boiler; cook over hot water until tender. Add blueberries and butter to rice, stirring slightly to mix. Beat eggs until light; add sugar, vanilla, salt, and remaining milk and beat until mixed, then stir into hot rice mixture. Pour into casserole, and sprinkle with cinnamon (or nutmeg.) Set casserole dish in larger pan, and fill this second pan half-full of hot water.

Bake for about 30 minutes, or until firmly set.

WINTER STEAMED PUDDING

INGREDIENTS

1½ cups dry-packed frozen blueberries

⅔ cup granulated sugar

⅓ cup butter or margarine, softened

2 eggs, at room temperature

2½ cups all-purpose flour

2½ teaspoons double-acting baking powder

¼ teaspoon salt

½ cup milk, at room temperature

TEMPERATURE

High for time it takes for steam to get under way; low for remainder of cooking time.

COOKING TIME

2½ hours on open stove (See manufacturer's directions for pressure cooker.)

NUMBER OF SERVINGS

6

Defrost blueberries enough to separate berries. Toss in small amount of flour to cover. Select a pudding mold with a tight cover; grease the inside well and sprinkle with sugar. Set a heavy kettle on the stove, with a trivet placed at bottom. (Kettle should be large enough to hold your mold, with space at sides, and should have a tight cover.) Start water to boil.

Cream butter and sugar together until the mix loses its granular appearance. Beat eggs thoroughly and add to the butter-sugar mixture. Sift flour and measure. Resift twice with baking powder, and salt. Add dry ingredients to the butter-egg-sugar mixture, alternating with milk, mixing after each addition. Fold in blueberries.

Pour batter into mold, filling to ⅔ capacity. Cover tightly. Unless you plan to steam your pudding in a pressure cooker (See manufacturer's directions), put the mold in the kettle, centering it carefully, and pour boiling water to a depth of one inch in bottom of kettle. Cover kettle tightly. Steam for two hours.

When ready to unmold, remove cover of mold and let steam escape before completely unmolding the pudding.

Serve hot with Hard Sauce or one of the other dessert sauces described on page 132.

COUSIN LAURA'S BLUEBERRY TRIFLE

INGREDIENTS
1 cup fresh blueberries
1-2 tablespoons confectioner's
sugar
1 cup stale cake cubes
(plain cake)
2 tablespoons rum
4 eggs, at room temperature
4 tablespoons granulated sugar
1½ cups hot milk
1 envelope unflavored gelatine
¾ cup heavy cream, cold
½ cup blanched, crushed
almonds
NUMBER OF SERVINGS
6

Wash, drain, and dry blueberries between paper towels. Toss in confectioner's sugar. Refrigerate while preparing rest of recipe.
Cut stale cake into cubes. Toss in the rum lightly. Separate eggs. Beat egg yolks with granulated sugar and gelatine. Pour hot milk over this. Cook in a saucepan until thickened, stirring continually, but be careful not to boil. When thickened, take from heat and stir over a bowl of ice until almost set. Beat egg whites until stiff. Whip cream until it forms peaks. Fold egg whites, whipped cream, and cake cubes into the egg-gelatine mixture. Then very gently, fold in ½ cup blueberries Spoon the mixture into six custard cups. Refrigerate cups for several hours.

When ready to serve, sprinkle tops of the cups with almonds. Trim with fresh mint leaves, and remainder of whole berries.

THICK STEWED BLUEBERRIES

INGREDIENTS
2 quarts fresh or dry-packed
frozen blueberries
1¼ cups granulated sugar
3 tablespoons cornstarch
½ teaspoon cinnamon
2 cups Sour Cream Sauce or
Custard Sauce
(See following pages.)
AMOUNT PRODUCED
About 3 pints or
8-10 servings
COOKING TIME
About 25 minutes

Wash and drain blueberries, or partially defrost to separate berries. Combine with sugar and 1½ cups water in a saucepan. Bring to a boil, stirring all the while. Reduce heat and simmer for seven minutes. Blend cornstarch with ¼ cup cold water, and add to the simmering berries, stirring to mix. Cook for about five minutes, until cornstarch is completely dissolved. Stir in cinnamon.
Serve with one of the recommended sauces, or with thick cream.

BLUEBERRY-STUFFED APPLES

INGREDIENTS
½ cup blueberries, fresh or
dry-packed frozen
6 whole tart cooking apples
¼ cup slivered almonds
6 tablespoons honey
6 teaspoons shredded coconut
3 tablespoons lemon juice
6 teaspoons butter or margarine
½ teaspoon cinnamon
OVEN TEMPERATURE
400°
BAKING TIME
About 45 minutes
NUMBER OF SERVINGS
6

Preheat oven to 400°. Wash, drain, and dry blueberries between paper towels. Wash and core apples. Pare them one-third of way down from top. Arrange apples in buttered baking dish. Mix blueberries, almonds, honey, coconut, and lemon juice together. Stuff each apple case with some of the fruit mixture. Top each stuffed apple with a teaspoon of butter. Give each a dash of cinnamon. Pour ½ cup water around apples to prevent sticking. Bake, uncovered, until tender — about 45 minutes.
Serve "as is", or with cream.

BLUEBERRY COEUR A LA CRÉME

INGREDIENTS	
½ cup fresh or dry-packed frozen blueberries	At least one-half hour before preparing this dish, set out cream cheese to soften at room temperature. Wash, drain, and dry blueberries between paper towels, if necessary, or defrost frozen berries enough to separate.

INGREDIENTS

½ cup fresh or dry-packed
frozen blueberries
Granddaddy's Bourbon-Laced
Blueberry Sauce
(See page 129)
2 cups small-curd
cottage cheese
1 cup soft cream cheese
½ cup light cream
⅓ cup granulated sugar
1 teaspoon grated lemon rind
⅛ teaspoon salt
1 envelope unflavored gelatine
1 teaspoon lemon juice
NUMBER OF SERVINGS
6

At least one-half hour before preparing this dish, set out cream cheese to soften at room temperature. Wash, drain, and dry blueberries between paper towels, if necessary, or defrost frozen berries enough to separate. In electric blender, beat the cottage cheese until it is soft. Add softened cream cheese, and continue beating until mixture is smoothly blended. Add cream, sugar, lemon rind, and salt. Soften gelatine in 2 tablespoons of cold water, and dissolve over hot water. Add gelatine and lemon juice to mixture in blender and mix thoroughly. When thoroughly blended, pour into 6 small heart-shaped molds or Mary Ann pans. (You'll want a depression in center of each mold.) Chill thoroughly for several hours.

Prepare Granddaddy's Bourbon-Laced Blueberry Sauce (Page 129). When ready to serve, turn Coeur à la Crèmes over on individual saucers. Spoon sauce in center depression of each mold, just enough to fill. Add whole blueberries to the remaining sauce and ladle around the edges of the crèmes.

Ice Cream, Ices, and Sherbet

BLUEBERRY ICE CREAM

So you don't think you'd like it? I didn't either until I passed that store that advertises the "32 flavors," and took a chance on one of their cones. I couldn't extract their recipe from them, but I came home and tried one of my own. M-m-m-m! Very good! After all, we have raspberry and blackberry creams and sherbet — why not blueberry, with its unique flavor and surprising color? I do definitely recommend that you try to get wild blueberries for this type of dessert, however, for their flavor is stronger and sweeter and less elusive than the commercial berries when combined with frosty ingredients.

BUTCH'S FAVORITE BLUEBERRY ICE CREAM

INGREDIENTS
1 quart fresh blueberries
1 cup granulated sugar
(Approx.)
Juice of half a lemon
2 cups thin cream, at
room temperature
Dash of salt
FREEZING TIME
4 hours
NUMBER OF SERVINGS
About 8

Wash blueberries quickly under running water and drain. Combine with sugar in a saucepan. Stew just until berries are soft and sugar is dissolved. Take from stove. Add dash of salt and the lemon juice. Mix, then mash. Strain through a medium coarse sieve. Let stand until cool. Add cream and mix. Taste for sweetness. Add more sugar (or corn syrup), if desired. Pour into trays and freeze to mushlike consistency. Remove to chilled bowl and beat until smooth, but not melted. Return to trays and complete freezing. This recipe makes about 1½ quarts.

ICES AND SHERBETS

Ices and sherbets are made in much the same way as ice cream. These desserts are delicious by themselves on a summer evening. They also add zest to salads and fruit desserts. They're tasty additions to fruit drinks or light punches. They may be served as appetizers (just add a sprig of mint and two or three fresh blueberries for eye-appeal). They make nice side dishes to serve in small portions with meat entrées.

Either fresh or canned blueberries may be used in such recipes.

MEGAN'S YUMMY SHERBET

INGREDIENTS
1 large can blueberries
1 cup granulated sugar
Juice of one lemon
2 envelopes unflavored gelatine
½ cup thick whipping cream, cold
FREEZING TIME
4 to 5 hours
NUMBER OF SERVINGS
About 8

Boil blueberries and sugar in two cups of water for about five minutes. Sprinkle gelatine on ½ cup cold water to soften. Dissolve gelatine in blueberry mixture. Add lemon juice and mix. Let stand until cool. Pour into trays and freeze to mush stage. Whip cream and set aside in refrigerator until needed. When berry mixture has reached the mush stage, remove from trays to a chilled bowl and beat until smooth. Fold in the whipped cream. Return to trays and complete freezing. This recipe makes about 1½ quarts.

GWYN'S BLUEBERRY ICE

INGREDIENTS
2 quarts fresh blueberries
1 cup granulated sugar
4 tablespoons lemon juice
1 cup of water
FREEZING TIME
4 to 5 hours; best left overnight
NUMBER OF SERVINGS
About 8

Purée blueberries in electric blender. Boil sugar and water together for five minutes. Cool. Combine blueberries and sugar-water mixture. Add lemon juice. Taste for sweetness or tartness. Add more sugar or lemon juice, if needed.
Put in freezer trays and freeze to a mush. Stir occasionally during freezing time to achieve a smoother blend.

LEMON-BLUEBERRY ICE

INGREDIENTS
1½ cups blueberry sauce
3 strips lemon rind
⅓ cup lemon juice
FREEZING TIME
4 hours or more
NUMBER OF SERVINGS
6

Make Blueberry Sauce according to directions on page 129. If kept ready in refrigerator, use as is. If freshly made and hot, cool to room temperature. Place lemon rind and lemon juice in electric blender and grind. Add Blueberry Sauce. Blend smooth. Taste for sweetness, and adjust accordingly. Place in refrigerator trays and freeze. Stir occasionally to help break up ice crystals. When about frozen, remove from trays to a chilled bowl and beat smooth (but not to melt). Return to ice trays and freeze until needed.

NOTE: If in a hurry, combine sauce with a can of frozen lemonade concentrate and 2 cans of water. Proceed as above.

Hybrid

BLUEBERRY PARFAIT

INGREDIENTS
3 cups fresh or dry-packed
frozen blueberries
¾ cup granulated sugar
1 tablespoon cornstarch
1 tablespoon lemon juice
dash each of salt,
cloves, cinnamon
1 quart ice cream

NUMBER OF SERVINGS
8

Wash blueberries quickly under running cold water and drain. Blend cornstarch, sugar, and salt in a saucepan. Stir in blueberries, spices and lemon juice. Cover and bring to a boil. Simmer for 12 minutes. Cool. Alternate blueberry mixture and ice cream in layers in parfait glasses, beginning with a generous dollop of the blueberry mixture at the bottom of the glass, ending with top layer of ice cream. Decorate with whipped cream and/or a sprig of mint and several sugared whole, large fresh berries.

Many flavors of commercial or homemade ice cream combine pleasingly with blueberries to make a variety of attractive and tasty desserts. For most of these, I prefer vanilla ice cream because of the blueberry's delicate flavor, but other flavors such as banana, frozen custard, coffee, eggnog, and butterscotch do well, too.

Of course, the simplest, and quite possibly the most popular of these dishes is the plain old ice cream sundae, which relies on its covering sauce for its distinctive flavor.

BLUEBERRY SUNDAE

INGREDIENTS
Blueberry Sauce
1 pint ice cream

NUMBER OF SERVINGS
2 to 4, depending upon the
size of appetites

Make one of the blueberry sauces described on pages 129-130. If this has been refrigerated previously for such use, warm in quantities needed in small saucepan and pour over individual servings of ice cream. This will taste surprisingly like Blueberry Jubilee (which follows) and is much quicker and easier to prepare.

UNCLE RASCAL'S SASSY BLUEBERRY JUBILEE

INGREDIENTS
1 large can blueberries
⅓ cup granulated sugar
2 tablespoons cornstarch
¼ cup brandy or
blackberry liqueur
1 quart ice cream
NUMBER OF SERVINGS
8

Drain blueberries, reserving syrup. Set both aside. Blend cornstarch and sugar in saucepan over medium heat. Gradually add reserved blueberry syrup, mixing well. Stir until mixture thickens and bubbles. Remove from heat. Stir in the drained berries. Fill lower pan in chafing dish with hot water. Light flame. Turn blueberry mixture into top chafing dish pan; keep hot over flame. Prepare ice cream in serving dishes.

Heat brandy in large ladle or small metal pan with long handle. Dim lights in room where jubilee is to be served; ignite heated brandy in front of guests and pour over blueberry mixture. Stir. Ladle blueberry-brandy sauce over ice cream and serve immediately.

PATRIOT'S SUNDAE

INGREDIENTS
1 serving of vanilla ice cream
3 teaspoons large
fresh blueberries
6 to 8 large, fresh strawberries
3 tablespoons marshmallow
sauce
NUMBER OF SERVINGS
One (Multiply ingredients by
number of servings needed.)

Top ice cream with marshmallow sauce. Sprinkle over this the strawberries and blueberries. Serve on Fourth of July, Washington's Birthday, or other patriotic occasion, with Patriot's Cake (See page 90).

Candies

BLUEBERRY CANDIES

These candy recipes are just a fun thing, and if you've your own blueberry field and lots of time, you might like to tackle them. The first offers one more suggestion for a way to use dried blueberries.

BLUEBERRY NUT ROLL

INGREDIENTS
½ pound dried blueberries
½ pound broken pecan meats
¼ pound candied lemon peel
½ teaspoon lemon juice
1 cup confectioner's sugar
AMOUNT PRODUCED
1½ pounds, or about
1½ dozen candies

Grind the berries, nut and lemon peel through the coarse cutter of your meat grinder. Mix in the lemon juice. Shape into balls about 1 inch in diameter. Roll in confectioner's sugar. Wrap in aluminum foil and chill before serving.

GLACÉED BLUEBERRIES

INGREDIENTS
1 cup woods-clean, firm,
whole blueberries
2 cups granulated sugar
⅛ teaspoon cream of tartar
1 cup boiling water
PREPARATION TIME
About one hour
AMOUNT PRODUCED
Half a pound

Sort the blueberries, but *don't* wash them. Try to drain any outer moisture off the berries by spreading on paper towels. Over low heat, in top of double boiler, dissolve sugar and cream of tartar in one cup of boiling water. Bring mixture to boiling point. Wash sides of pan down occasionally with pastry brush dipped in ice water. Cook to hard-crack stage as indicated on your candy thermometer. Meanwhile, make sure there is hot water in the bottom of the double boiler. When syrup has reached the hard-crack stage, remove from stove, dip pan for just a moment in cold water, then place over the bottom part of the double boiler.

Quickly dip berries into hot syrup a few at a time, removing with a fork to a sheet of waxed paper to cool. Serve same day they are made, for they will not keep.

Highbush

Beverages

BLUEBERRY BEVERAGES

Some delightful drinks, both fermented and nonalcoholic, can be prepared with blueberries. For the lucky person with access to large wild blueberry plants, this need not be an extravagant endeavor.

The following recipes for blueberry wines were sent me by the Cooperative Extension Service, U.S. Department of Agriculture, University of New Hampshire, in Durham.

BLUEBERRY WINE

INGREDIENTS
4 quarts of wild or
domestic blueberries
8 cups cane sugar
1 slice of whole wheat toast
1 ounce of wet yeast
4 quarts of water
AMOUNT PRODUCED
About 8 quarts

If the woods where you pick the berries are cool and clean, do not wash berries; but if they are gritty and dusty, rinse quickly under cold running water. Then put them into canner kettle, and mash thoroughly with a potato masher. Bring 2 quarts of the water to a boil, along with the sugar. Boil for 5 minutes, then pour over berries. This will set the red-purple color.

Add the other two quarts of cool water and stir well. Moisten yeast with a few drops of water and spread on the toast. Float the toast, yeast side down, on the surface of the liquid. Put in a warm place to ferment for two weeks. Stir gently from the bottom every day during this period.

Then strain through a jelly bag, squeezing pulp very dry to extract all of the color and flavor. Return to canner kettle to settle for two days. Then siphon off into clean sterilized bottles and cork lightly.

This wine takes about three weeks to finish fermenting in the bottle, so don't be too eager to fasten the corks tightly. When fermentation has ceased, cork tightly and seal with paraffin.

Keep for at least six months; but if you wait a year the body and color of the wine will greatly improve.

BLUEBERRY-CHERRY WINE

INGREDIENTS
(first 2 weeks)
3 quarts blueberries
3 quarts black-ripe Bing cherries
4 quarts water, at room temperature
INGREDIENTS
(second 2 weeks)
8 cups of cane sugar
2 large shredded wheat biscuits or 1 cup Wheat Chex
1 package dry granulated yeast
AMOUNT PRODUCED
About 10 quarts

Combine blueberries and cherries in the canner kettle and mash with potato masher until fine. Be careful not to break the cherry pits, as they will give the wine a bitter taste. Add the room temperature water, and set in a warm place to ferment for two weeks.

At end of this time, strain through jelly bag, squeezing well to extract all of the flavor and liquid. Reserve 2 cups of liquid for dissolving the sugar; return the rest to the canner kettle. Dissolve the sugar in the 2 cups of liquid over a low flame; bring to a boil for 5 minutes. While still hot, add to the liquid in the canner kettle. Crumble the shredded wheat and add; if using Wheat Chex, add them as they come from the box. Stir well to circulate the sugar and the wheat; then sprinkle the dry granulated yeast over the surface. Set in a warm place to ferment for two weeks without disturbing.

At end of second 2-week period, strain through several thicknesses of cheesecloth and return to the canner kettle to settle for two days more. Siphon off into clean sterilized bottles and cork lightly until fermentation has ceased. When fermentation is over, cork tightly and seal with paraffin. Keep for six months.

For those who prefer a nonalcoholic drink, I recommend the following recipe. This makes a most refreshing base for a summer drink. In winter, you may wish to add that certain warming fillip contained in a "medicinal" shot of rum or bourbon.

GRANDMA'S BLUEBERRY SHRUB

INGREDIENTS
6 quarts fresh or dry-packed
frozen blueberries
1 quart cider vinegar
3 pounds granulated sugar
(Approx.)
NUMBER OF SERVINGS
32

If you use wild blueberries from woods that are clean and cool, do not wash the berries, but if they are gritty and dusty, rinse quickly under cold, running water, and drain. Mash berries and place them in a large crock. Cover with vinegar. Let stand for a day and a night, then crush berries once more, and squeeze them through a jelly bag, or improvised bag of double cheesecloth, into a large kettle.

For each quart of juice you extract, add two pounds of sugar. Bring to a boil and simmer until sugar dissolves. Taste for sweetness, adding more sugar. if you wish.

When cool, pour into sterile bottles or jars, cap, and refrigerate until ready to use.

This will make about one quart of shrub. May be served over shaved ice, or combined with soft drinks such as ginger ale.

SMALL FRY'S BIG SHAKE

INGREDIENTS
1 small can blueberry pie filling
1 pint vanilla ice cream
2 cups cold milk
Dash of cinnamon
AMOUNT PRODUCED
2-4 thick shakes

Pour pie filling into electric blender with milk and cinnamon. Blend until thick and fluffy. Add ice cream one-half at a time. Follow each addition by blending for 6 seconds. Pour into tall glasses. Serve with straw and iced teaspoon.

Syrup, Glazes, and Sauces

BLUEBERRY SYRUP

INGREDIENTS
1 cup blueberries, fresh
or frozen
¼ cup granulated sugar
¼ cup water
Dash of cinnamon
AMOUNT PRODUCED
About 1 cupful

Wash and drain berries, if necessary. Combine ingredients and bring to a boil. Crush berries with the back of a spoon. Simmer 2 to 3 minutes. Serve hot. Especially good with pancakes. Add a jigger of brandy, gin, or blackberry liqueur and you've a sensational sauce to serve over cold, whole blueberries and/or ice cream.

RELIABLE BLUEBERRY GLAZE

INGREDIENTS
2 cups fresh blueberries
1 cup granulated sugar
¼ cup water
1½ tablespoons cornstarch
Dash of salt
1 teaspoon butter
AMOUNT PRODUCED
2-3 cupfuls

Wash blueberries and crush one cupful, setting other aside. In small saucepan combine crushed berries, sugar, water, cornstarch, and salt. Cook over medium heat, stirring constantly until thickened. Cook two additional minutes. Stir in butter. Put through strainer. Cool glaze slightly before using. Stir in second cup of whole berries just before serving. Principally used on cheesecake.

QUICK BLUEBERRY GLAZE — I

INGREDIENTS
1¾ cups dry-packed
frozen blueberries
1 package (3 oz.)
blackberry gelatine
1 cup boiling water
AMOUNT PRODUCED
About 2½ cupfuls

Dissolve gelatine in boiling water. Add frozen blueberries and stir until berries separate and mixture thickens. Spoon over cheesecake. Chill until firm.

QUICK BLUEBERRY GLAZE — II

INGREDIENTS
1 large can blueberries
½ teaspoon lemon juice
1 tablespoon butter
1½ tablespoons cornstarch
AMOUNT PRODUCED
2-3 cupfuls

Drain blueberries. Pour juice into saucepan. Add lemon juice and butter; stir to mix. Add cornstarch; stir to mix. Cook over medium heat, stirring constantly until juice thickens. Cook two additional minutes. Add berries. Cool slightly before using.

MAPLE SYRUP GLAZE

(To top good blueberry dishes!)
INGREDIENTS
1 3-oz. package
unflavored gelatine
1 cup maple syrup
¼ cup boiling water
1 teaspoon butter
AMOUNT PRODUCED
About 1 cupful

Dissolve gelatine in water. Add maple syrup and butter and stir over medium heat until mixture thickens. Cool slightly before using.

GRANDDADDY'S BOURBON-LACED BLUEBERRY SAUCE

INGREDIENTS
2 cups fresh blueberries
½ cup granulated sugar
1 teaspoon grated lemon rind
Dash of salt
2 tablespoons all-purpose flour
¼ teaspoon each of cinnamon,
nutmeg, and allspice
¼ cup bourbon
AMOUNT PRODUCED
2 cupfuls

Combine flour with ¼ cup water. Heat blueberries, sugar, lemon rind. Stir until sugar is melted. Add flour mixture, stirring and cooking until thick. Remove sauce from heat. Stir in spices. Cool. Add bourbon, pour into a jar or crock, cover and let set for several hours, Serve hot or cold. (Note: Granddaddy used rice flour instead of all-purpose flour. Said it gave his sauce an unusual texture. If your store supplies it, you might like to try it. It is not always easy to find.)

QUICK AND EASY BLUEBERRY SAUCE

INGREDIENTS
2 cups fresh or dry-packed
frozen blueberries
½ cup granulated sugar
1 tablespoon lemon juice or
1 teaspoon grated lemon rind
1 tablespoon cornstarch
Dash of salt
COOKING TIME
About 5 minutes
AMOUNT PRODUCED
About 1 cupful

Wash and drain blueberries. In a saucepan, combine blueberries, sugar, lemon juice, and ½ cup of water. Bring to a boil, then lower heat and cook for 3 to 5 minutes, stirring slowly. Taste for adjustments in amounts of sugar and lemon. Add salt. Mix cornstarch thoroughly in half cup cold water; pour into hot blueberry mixture. Boil for a minute or two until sauce thickens.
Serve hot or cold over desserts, pancakes, or waffles. Very good over steamed blueberry pudding.

SPICY BLUEBERRY SAUCE

Use recipe for Quick and Easy Blueberry Sauce (page 129). Add a bag containing a cinnamon stick and several whole cloves, boiling along with the first ingredients, removing from saucepan just before adding cornstarch.

When ready to remove sauce from heat, add two tablespoons kirsch, blackberry liqueur, sherry, rum, or other alcoholic flavoring, if you wish.

OLD-TIMER'S BLUEBERRY GAME SAUCE

INGREDIENTS
1 cup dried blueberries*
(See page 21)
1 cup port wine
1 tablespoon butter
1 tablespoon flour
½ to 1 cup Blueberry-Apple Jelly (See page 138)
Dash of salt
AMOUNT PRODUCED
About 2 cupfuls

Heat the berries in port wine until they puff up. Add jelly and stir to mix. Add butter and flour a little at a time, stirring occasionally until mixture thickens. Add dash of salt. Serve with boiled beef, wild or domestic game.
*You can use fresh wild berries; if you do, heat just to warm through.

SAUCES AND FILLINGS THAT GO WELL WITH BLUEBERRY DISHES

The following sauces have been mentioned in recipes throughout this book. They are included for your convenience. You may prefer to use favorites of your own.

ORANGE SAUCE

INGREDIENTS
⅔ cup granulated sugar
1¼ cups orange juice
3 tablespoons orange rind
2 tablespoons cornstarch
Dash of salt
2 tablespoons Cointreau or Triple Sec (optional)
AMOUNT PRODUCED
About 2 cupfuls

Grate orange rind. Cook sugar, orange juice, orange rind, and salt over low heat until sugar is melted. Mix cornstarch in ½ cup water, and add to other ingredients. Cook until thickened, stirring constantly. Remove from stove and cool slightly. Add liqueur, if desired.

LEMON SAUCE

INGREDIENTS
½ cup granulated sugar
2 tablespoons light corn syrup
1 tablespoon cornstarch
Dash each of salt and nutmeg
1 tablespoon lemon rind
Juice of one lemon
2 tablespoons soft butter
AMOUNT PRODUCED
1½ cupfuls

Grate lemon rind. Mix all ingredients *except butter and lemon juice* in a saucepan with ¼ cup of water. Boil, stirring lightly, until sauce is clear and thickened. Remove from heat and stir in butter and lemon juice.

MAPLE SYRUP SAUCE

INGREDIENTS
1 cup maple syrup
½ cup cream
⅛ teaspoon grated nutmeg
1 tablespoon butter
AMOUNT PRODUCED
1½ cupfuls
COOKING TIME
About 20 minutes

Boil maple syrup and cream to soft ball stage (234°-238° F.). Beat for one minute. Add vanilla and nutmeg, mixing well. If served hot, add butter and stir. Served cold, omit butter.

SOUR CREAM SAUCE

INGREDIENTS
1 pint commercial sour cream
1 teaspoon vanilla
¼ cup granulated sugar, or firm-packed light brown sugar
AMOUNT PRODUCED
1½ cupfuls

Whip cream to consistency of soft custard. Beat in other ingredients until well blended. Chill.

VANILLA SAUCE

INGREDIENTS
½ cup granulated sugar
1 tablespoon cornstarch
3 tablespoons butter
or margarine
Dash each of salt and nutmeg
1 teaspoon vanilla
COOKING TIME
5 minutes
AMOUNT PRODUCED
1 cupful

Mix sugar and cornstarch in small saucepan. Add one cup boiling water. Boil for five minutes, stirring constantly. Remove from heat. Stir in butter, vanilla, and seasonings.

CUSTARD SAUCE

INGREDIENTS
4 egg yolks
¼ cup granulated sugar
2 cups milk
½ teaspoon vanilla extract
Pinch of salt
AMOUNT PRODUCED
About 2 cupfuls

Beat egg yolks slightly and place in top of a double boiler. Add sugar and salt and mix well. Scald milk and add to mixture. Cook and stir over hot water until mixture thickens and coats a dry metal spoon. Pour into bowl and cool. Add vanilla, stirring to mix.

HARD SAUCE

INGREDIENTS
1 cup confectioner's sugar
4 tablespoons soft butter
1 teaspoon vanilla
¼ cup heavy cream, at
room temperature
Few grains of salt
AMOUNT PRODUCED
1 cup

Sift sugar. Beat butter until soft. Slowly add sugar to butter, beating until completely creamed and very light. Add vanilla very slowly. Add salt and mix. Beat in the cream until very smooth. Lightly transfer to serving dish. Chill before using, but do not freeze. (Should not be too hard when served.)

BRANDY SAUCE

INGREDIENTS
¼ cup softened butter
1 cup confectioner's sugar
2 large eggs, at
room temperature
½ cup cream, at
room temperature
3 tablespoons brandy
AMOUNT PRODUCED
2 cupfuls

Beat egg whites until stiff. Set aside. In another bowl, beat egg yolks until light. Cream butter and sugar until granular appearance disappears. Add egg yolks and cream to butter and sugar.
Cook in top of a double boiler, over hot water, stirring occasionally, until mixture is thickened and coats a dry metal spoon. Remove from stove and fold in egg whites. Add brandy.

FOAMY SAUCE

INGREDIENTS
1 cup confectioner's sugar
1 large egg
⅓ cup butter or margarine
2 tablespoon sherry
Dash of salt
COOKING TIME
10-15 minutes
AMOUNT PRODUCED
1 cup

Sift sugar. Separate egg, beating yolk and white separately, the latter until stiff. Cream butter until soft and fluffy, gradually beating in sugar until well blended, then the egg yolk, and the sherry.
Place in top of double boiler and beat over simmering water until sauce thickens. Fold in egg white and salt. Serve hot or cold.

NOTE: Three tablespoons orange juice, or 1 tablespoon vanilla or brandy may be substituted for sherry.

Frostings, Fillings, and Toppings

BLUEBERRY-CHEESE FROSTING

INGREDIENTS
2 cups fresh blueberries
1 8-ounce package cream cheese,
at room temperature
2 tablespoons cream, at
room temperature
2 tablespoons honey
AMOUNT PRODUCED
About 1 cupful

Wash, drain, and dry blueberries between paper towels. Crush blueberries and mix honey in with them. Beat the cream into the cream cheese until mixture is smooth. Mix in the blueberries.
Use as a frosting for any plain cake, or as a spread for bread, muffins, or between layers of cake.

MAPLE FROSTING

INGREDIENTS
2 cups confectioner's sugar
1 tablespoon butter, at
room temperature
Pinch of salt
4 tablespoons maple syrup
½ teaspoon vanilla
1 tablespoon heavy cream
(optional)
AMOUNT PRODUCED
1 cupful

Sift sugar. Combine sugar and all other ingredients. Beat until mixture is smooth and the right consistency to spread.

BUTTER FROSTING

INGREDIENTS
½ cup soft butter
2 cups confectioner's sugar
3 tablespoons milk (Approx.)
1 egg yolk
1 teaspoon vanilla
Pinch of salt

AMOUNT PRODUCED
Enough to cover 2 dozen cup
cakes or 1 large two-layer cake

Cream butter. Add one-half of the sugar, a little at a time, creaming after each addition, until mixture is light and fluffy. Beat in egg yolk. Add remaining sugar, alternating with milk, beating after each addition, until right consistency to spread. Add flavoring and salt, stirring to mix.

ORANGE BUTTER FILLING

INGREDIENTS
2 teaspoons grated orange rind
2 tablespoons soft butter
½ cup granulated sugar
2 tablespoons cornstarch
1 egg yolk, at
room temperature
Pinch of salt
½ cup orange juice
3 teaspoons lemon juice

COOKING TIME
About 20 minutes

AMOUNT PRODUCED
About 1 cup

Combine sugar and cornstarch, salt, and slightly beaten egg yolk in top of double boiler. Add orange juice, lemon juice, and one-half cup of water. Cook over direct heat, stirring constantly, until mixture comes to a boil. Set pan over bottom of double boiler containing hot water. Continue cooking for 12 minutes, stirring as needed. Add orange rind and butter. Mix and cool.

BLUEBERRY CRÉME CHANTILLY

INGREDIENTS
1 cup fresh blueberries
1 cup whipping cream, cold
2 tablespoons
confectioner's sugar (about)
1 teaspoon vanilla extract,
or rum

AMOUNT PRODUCED
About 1½ cups

Wash, drain blueberries, crush, and strain through a sieve. Have beater and bowl very cold. Beat cream until it doubles in volume. Mix in confectioner's sugar and vanilla or rum. Fold in blueberry pulp. Serve on cakes, puddings, grunts.

MAPLE BUTTER FILLING

INGREDIENTS
⅓ cup all-purpose flour
¾ cup granulated sugar
¼ teaspoon salt
2 eggs, at room temperature
2 cups milk, hot
2 tablespoons maple syrup
2 tablespoons butter
COOKING TIME
About 18 minutes
AMOUNT PRODUCED
About 2 cupfuls

Combine sugar, flour, and salt in top of double boiler. Partially fill bottom of double boiler with water and bring to a boil. Lightly mix eggs and combine with dry ingredients in top of double boiler (not yet placed over hot water). Scald milk. Pour small amount into the mixture prepared, and mix to a paste. Add rest of scalded milk. Place top section over bottom of double boiler. Boil for 5 minutes, stirring the mixture in the top continually. Continue to cook, stirring occasionally, until the mixture thickens (About 10 minutes). Cool. Add maple syrup and butter, stirring to mix.

THICK BLUEBERRY TOPPING

INGREDIENTS
1 quart fresh blueberries
⅔ cup granulated sugar
2 tablespoons lemon juice
½ tablespoon Angostura Bitters
COOKING TIME
5 minutes
AMOUNT PRODUCED
About 3 cupfuls

Combine all ingredients with half cup water in a stainless steel or enamel saucepan. Bring to a boil and cook for 5 minutes, stirring slowly all the while to prevent burning. Chill and serve cold with cakes or other desserts.

Jellies, Jams, and Pickles

Pectin is a natural carbohydrate with thickening properties found in differing amounts in fruits.

Blueberries are low in pectin. To make jellies of low-pectin fruits, they must be combined with high-pectin fruits, or with commercial pectins, or both, if they are to be firm enough to hold their shape. This is why you will find apples or cranberries, which are high in pectin, in most of the blueberry recipes which follow.

Commercial fruit pectins are made from apples or citrus fruits. They are sold in two forms, liquid and powdered. Either is satisfactory, when used in a recipe developed especially for that form.

It is wise to select *slightly* underripe blueberries when making jellies and jams, for they have more natural pectin in them at this stage than later. Wild blueberries will yield a better flavor, if you are fortunate enough to have access to them.

AUNT JOSIE'S BLUEBERRY JAM

INGREDIENTS
2 quarts fresh blueberries
6 cups granulated sugar
1 teaspoon each of cinnamon,
cloves, and allspice
1 cup liquid pectin
COOKING TIME
About 15 minutes
AMOUNT PRODUCED
About 8 pints

Wash blueberries and put in stainless steel or enamel kettle. Crush berries. Simmer. Add sugar and spices. Stir to dissolve. Bring to a boil. Add pectin, and continue to boil for two minutes. Remove from heat. Skim off foam, but do not stir. Pour, while still boiling hot, into hot, sterilized jars. Cover with paraffin. Cool for approximately 30 minutes. When completely cool, seal with cover, label, date, and store in cool, dark place.

BLUEBERRY-APPLE JELLY

INGREDIENTS
2 quarts fresh firm blueberries
3 pounds firm tart apples
7 cups granulated sugar
3 teaspoons lemon juice
1 package powdered pectin
COOKING TIME
Approximately 25 minutes
AMOUNT PRODUCED
4 pints

Get glasses or jars ready. Wash containers in warm, soapy water, and rinse in hot water, or put through sani-cycle of your dish-washing machine. Keep them hot — either in a slow oven or in hot water — until they are used. This will prevent containers from breaking when filled with hot jelly or jam. Treat caps and lids in the same way. If rings are used, wash in hot soapy water, and rinse well. Have your other utensils ready before you start.

Wash, drain, then mash blueberries. Wash apples, core, and cut in eighths (leave skins). Simmer apples in 4 cups of water for 15 minutes; mash. Drain and squeeze apples through a jelly bag. Simmer blueberries in half a cup of water for 7 minutes. Drain and squeeze apples through a jelly bag. Combine blueberry and apple juices (*not* pulp). You should have seven cupfuls. Add the sugar, then the lemon juice and pectin to these juices. Pour into a stainless steel or enamel kettle.

Bring to a rapid boil. Boil for 2 minutes, or until jelly thermometer registers 220°. Remove from heat. Skim froth from top of jelly. Pour into hot, sterilized jelly glasses to within ¼" of the rims. Seal with thin layer of melted paraffin, being sure that the paraffin touches all the way around the rim. Label and date. Store in a cool, dark area.

SPICED BLUEBERRY-PEACH CONSERVE

INGREDIENTS
1 quart fresh blueberries, or
two 10-ounce packages dry-
packed frozen blueberries
2 pounds fully-ripe peaches
2 tablespoons lemon juice
5½ cups granulated sugar
½ teaspoon salt
½ teaspoon each of cinnamon
and cloves

Boil a small amount of water and measure with a thermometer to assure your boiling point which may differ from others according to altitude. Wash peaches, peel, remove pits. Chop or grind peaches. Wash and drain blueberries. (Thaw, if frozen.) Measure 4 cups chopped peaches into a stainless steel kettle along with the blueberries and lemon juice. Cover,

¼ teaspoon whole allspice
COOKING TIME
Approximately half an hour
AMOUNT PRODUCED
4 pints

and bring to a boil, then reduce heat and simmer for 10 minutes, stirring occasionally to prevent sticking along sides. Add sugar and salt, stirring well. Tie spices in cloth bag and add to kettle.
Boil rapidly, stirring constantly, to 9 degrees above boiling point of water. (If you do not have a jelly thermometer, boil until mixture thickens.) Remove from heat and take out spices. Skim foam, but do not stir.

Pour, while still boiling hot, into hot, sterilized jars. Seal with paraffin. Cool for about 30 minutes (pint jars), then, if fruit has risen, shake jars to distribute the berries through the syrup. When completely cool, cap, label, date, and store in a cool, dark place.

Lowbush

BLUEBERRY MARMALADE

INGREDIENTS
1 quart fresh blueberries
3 cups granulated sugar
1 orange
1 lemon
3 ounces liquid pectin
AMOUNT PRODUCED
6 half-pint jars

Sterilize jars to be used. Wash, drain, and crush blueberries. Combine berries with sugar and 2 cups of water. Bring to a boil, then simmer for 15 minutes. Stir occasionally. Wash orange and lemon thoroughly. Grate rinds of both, and extract juice. Add rinds and juice to the blueberries. Bring to a rolling boil and boil for one minute. Remove from stove and add liquid pectin. Skim off foam. Continue to stir and skim until there is no more foam (About 5 minutes). Pour into hot, dry, sterilized jars, filling to within $\frac{1}{4}$-inch of the top. Cool until marmalade has set. Then cover with thin layer of hot melted paraffin. When paraffin is cool, add another thin layer. Top jar, if you wish. Then label and store in a cool, dark, dry place.

BLUEBERRY PICKLES

"Blueberry PICKLES!!" everyone screeched at me when I told my friends there would be such a recipe in my blueberry cookbook. "Nobody ever made *pickles* out of BLUEBERRIES!"

Well, they did and I do, and they're very good, too. And just to prove that it's no innovation of mine but an established idea of long-standing, I've always pointed out to such disbelievers the following recipe which I found in an old cookbook that belonged to my grandmother, *The Household Gem Cyclopedia,* published in the year 1891.

I hope you won't take the "receipt," as it was called, seriously, but everyone to whom I showed it insisted that I include it in my collection, "Just to give the book a light touch! *Must* all cookbooks be so depressingly orthodox all of the time?" So — here it is — somebody's dear old granny's forthright description of a no-nonsense way to make the best of what one has:

BLUE-BERRY PICKLES

"For blue-berry pickles, old jars which have lost their covers, or whose edges have been broken so that the covers will not fit tightly, serve an excellent purpose, as these pickles must not be kept air-tight.

"Pick over your berries, using only sound ones; fill your jars or wide-mouthed bottles to within an inch of the top, then pour in molasses enough to settle down into all spaces; this cannot be done in a moment, as molasses does not run very freely. Only lazy people will feel obliged to stand by and watch its progress. As it settles, pour in more until the berries are covered. Then tie over the top a piece of cotton cloth to keep the flies and other insects out, and set away in a preserve closet. Cheap molasses is good enough, and your pickles will soon be 'sharp.'"

GRANDMOTHER ROBINSON'S PICKLED BLUEBERRIES

INGREDIENTS
1 quart fresh blueberries
½ teaspoon nutmeg
2 teaspoons salt
4 cups cider vinegar
¾ cup honey
3 tablespoons molasses
AMOUNT PRODUCED
5 pints

Wash and drain blueberries. Put berries in a large crock. Mix all other ingredients and pour over berries. Let stand for three or more days until drawn juice covers blueberries. Stir to mix, then pour into sterilized jars and seal, label, and date.

BLUEBERRY RELISH

INGREDIENTS
2 quarts fresh blueberries
1 large onion
½ pound seedless raisins
½ cup brown sugar
1 pint cider vinegar
1 teaspoon each of ginger,
cinnamon, and mustard
Dash of salt
Few grains of cayenne pepper
AMOUNT PRODUCED
4 pints

Slice onion. Put in electric blender with blueberries and raisins, a little at a time, using the speed for chopping. Remove to a stainless steel or enamel vessel. Add all other ingredients. Mix and simmer until thickened. Pour into hot, sterilized jars and cool before covering. Label and date. Store in a cool, dark place for about six weeks before using.

Yogurt with Blueberries

A number of people have asked me whether I intended to include a blueberry yogurt recipe in this book.

For my part, making yogurt isn't worth the time and patience it requires, although, with the new electric yogurt machines and brewing jars, it's easier and more fun than formerly. For those who eat yogurt regularly, making one's own is certainly cheaper and more satisfactory. For the occasional sampler, a commercially-prepared package is usually handier. I do think that yogurt makes an enjoyable low-calorie dessert, main luncheon dish, or between-times snack, and is especially tasty when mixed with blueberries.

Blueberry-Yogurt can be purchased in convenient packages, but I believe that if you have *fresh, wild* blueberries readily available, you'll double your enjoyment if you purchase or make plain yogurt and use your own berries with it. You can mix the two together, or serve the one on top of the other. I like to add a little lemon juice either to the one or the other when I do this. Sometimes I serve a blueberry-yogurt dressing on fruit salads, particularly those with citrus fruits. Yogurt is very good with blueberry soups, too (See page 58).

After All

If you have read this far, I trust you have been tempted to stop more than once to try a recipe that particularly appealed to you. I sincerely hope that you found the preparation easy and the eating good, and that these pages have stimulated your interest in the blueberry as a plant and blueberries as an increasingly important American industry.

It is midsummer now, and in the fields the blueberries are swollen and round, but not yet blue for picking. So, while your mouth is still watering from reading about all the goodies represented by these recipes, decide to visit New Hampshire where wild blueberries grow on many sunny slopes, where the mountain air is clean and pure, where there's still space for roaming and time left for dreaming.

The Author

Index

GENERAL INDEX

Shakers, 6
Smith, Peter, 23
Sooy, Ezekiel, 8-9
State universities, 12
Sugar-pack method, 19
Syrup-pack method, 19

Trackleberry, 5

U.S. Department of Agriculture,
   ix, 7, 9, 10, 12

Vitamins in blueberries, 22

Western evergreen
   blueberries, 14-15
Weymouth blueberries, 14
Whinberry, 5
White, Elizabeth C., 8
Whortle berries, 5
Wyeth, Andrew, 11

Yogurt with blueberries, 142

RECIPE INDEX

Notes for Cooks

Notes

Notes

Notes